AN URGENT MESSAGE FOR HUMANITY

Glucose
- Alpha lipoic
- gluco (pure sio)

HORM
Agnus cast

Dig. ENZ.
+ HCL

LUTEOLIN + PEA } Bulimoss
Clinic paper   }

AN URGENT MESSAGE FOR HUMANITY

Received During A Groundbreaking Scientific Mediumship Research Project from the Spirit Realm

Bigelow Institute of Consciousness Studies Challenge Grant Recipient

FINAL REPORT

FOREWORD

Raymond Moody, MD, PhD

FOREWORD

Col. (R) John Alexander, PhD

INSTITUTE FOR THE SCIENTIFIC STUDY OF CONSCIOUSNESS

ALL RIGHTS RESERVED under Title 17, U.S. Code, International, and Pan-American Copyright Conventions. The duplication, sharing, uploading, transfer, and distribution of this electronic book by any digital, electronic, or printed process without the publisher's explicit permission is unauthorized.

PRODUCED BY:
Institute For The Scientific Study of Consciousness
BICS Challenge Grant Recipient

isscusa.org

First Edition 2024
Copyright © ISSC 2024.
All Rights Reserved

PUBLISHED BY:

GRAPEVINE BOOKS
ajparrbooks@gmail.com

Dedicated to Robert Bigelow: A True Pioneer and Visionary

"The spirit world has presented an urgent message for us: We are at a crossroads in human development. Our failures to love one another have escalated to the point where we face self-extinction.

"The message is urgent and unmistakable. It is easy to ignore, as we have been presented with so many scenarios of doom and gloom, from nuclear holocausts to warnings from scientists about climate change incompatible with human life, over the past decades.

"Consider this: Robert Bigelow funded this inquiry into the spiritual world concerning humanity's seemingly lack of spiritual progress over the past 150-plus years. We presented these questions as numbers, so the mediums could not know what the questions were asking to 19 different mediums living in various areas of the United States. All nineteen mediums were unanimous in transmitting this urgent and surprising message to humanity: Learn to love or face extinction."

Dr. Melvin Morse. ISSC

2024: ISSC Partakes in Ground-Breaking Mediumship Research

Funded by the Bigelow Institute for Consciousness Studies

WHAT ARE THE FOUR BICS QUESTIONS?

QUESTION 1:

"Since 1857, has the Other Side failed and Mankind failed to achieve good progress in securing human spirituality? If so, are bad spirits and bad humans winning?
(given to the mediums as 621055219)

QUESTION 2:

Explain to people on Earth why the Other Side has not failed in fostering spiritual evolution. *(given to the mediums as 292846648)*

QUESTION 3:

What difference has the Other Side made in the past 166 years in influencing humans to accelerate their spiritual progress? *(given to the mediums as 879610310)*

QUESTION 4:

To what extent have earthbound spirits since 1857 impeded, sabotaged, or distorted the progress of human spiritual evolution? *(given to the mediums as 106261065)*

Six scientific teams were chosen out of over 400 applications. Their mission was to interview mediums to assess the current state of the progress of humanity's spiritual development. This is the final report of our findings to BICS.

TABLE OF CONTENTS

Foreword by Raymond Moody, MD 1
Foreword by Col (R) John Alexander 5
   Dr. Morse's innovative research 6
   The current changing scientific paradigm 7
About the Study by Melvin Morse, MD 9
   Why We Presented The BICS Questions As Numbers 11
   We Set The Standards For Mediumship 13
Evaluation of the Mediums 17
   Filiation data 18
   Psychological profile 21
   Factors related to dissociation 23
Allan Kardec's 1857 Study 25
   Consulting Multiple Spirits 26
   The Science Behind Kardec's Research 27
   Kardec's Main Conclusions 27
BICS Challenge Final Report 31
I.- Abstract 33
II.- Introduction 37
   Who is ISSC? 37
   Why is this Study Important? 39
III.- Experimental Design and Methods 41
   The Mediums and Entities Contacted 41
      The Selection of Mediums 41
      The Presentation of the Questions 45
      Who are the Mediums? 46
      Blinded versus Nonblinded sessions 49

Psychiatric Assessment of the Mediums 50
The Entities 50
Summary of Entities Contacted 52
Table One: Information about Mediums 54
How Were the Medium Sessions Assessed? 57
Did the Mediums Contact Discarnate Entities? 61
TOS Presented Validation Within the Information Presented 64
IV Results 69
A.- BICS Question One: Answers 69
   A1.- Yes and No Answers 69
   Consensus Viewpoint 69
   A2.- Progress Through Failure 70
   A3.- Humans Are Failing 71
   A4: Humans Have Not Failed 72
   A5.- Human Progress is Non-Linear 73
   A6.- Human Progress is Cyclical 74
   A7.-Allan Kardec's Views on the Matter 74
   The Risk of Self-Inflicted Extinction (Supplemental Question 2) 75
   Remedies: Supplemental Question 2 76
B.- BICS Question Two: Answers 78
   B1.- No One has Failed 78
   B2.- Mankind has Failed to Listen to TOS 79
   B3.- How the Other Side Has Helped 80
   B4.- Connection With the Other Side 83
   B5.- What Allan Kardec Said 84
C.- BICS Question Three: Answers 85

C1.- Influence on Science and Technology 85
  C2.- What Allan Kardec Said...90
  C3.- Role of Death In Spiritual Progress: 90
  C4.- What Allan Kardec Said: 92
 D.- BICS Question Four: Answers......................................93
  D1.- Defining Earthbound Spirits and Their Role 93
  D2.- Negative Influence of These Spirits 96
  D3.- Positive Influence of These Spirits 97
  D4.- Human Choices and Free Will:..................................98
  D5. What Allan Kardec Said..100
  D6.- Communication With the Other Side......................100
  D7.- What Allan Kardec Said 101
  Table 2: The Mediums Answers to the Questions 102
  E.- Importance of the BICS Project 104
V.- Discussion 107
 Question 1: Assessed as one Long Conversation with TOS ..108
 Questions 2 and 3: A Timeline of the Answers 113
  TOS's Opening Statement to the BICS Jury...................114
  Specifics are Now Given 115
  More Examples 115
  Remedies...115
  Next: More Advanced Concepts 117
  The Other Side's Closing Statement 118
 Question 3 Discussion 119
  What Allan Kardec Said 120
VI.- Conclusion 121
VII Additional Background and Context 125

x

Glossary 125
Research Background 126
The Semmelweis Effect: "I Just Do not Believe It" 127
Mediumship and the Science of the 21st Century 128
Matter no Longer Matters. 129
Kuhn Paradigm Shift Cycle Stage 3: Crisis 130
The Science of Mediumship 130
   1.- Death is Just a Body Problem 131
   2.- "Information is the Only Thing that Exists" 132
   3.- The Brain as a Read-Write Head of Information 133
   4.- Top-Down Causation and a Conscious Universe 133
   5.- The Soul is a Cluster Of Information 134
   6.- The Brain is an Antenna 134
  Wet, Warm Brains are Capable of Quantum Processes 136
VIII.- References **137**
Appendix **149**
Additional BICS Questions 1 .... **151**
  SQ 1| 151
   On Help Received in the Last 100 Years 151
  SQ 2 152
   On Self-Extinction and Remedies 152
  SQ 3 153
  SQ 4 153
   On the Other Side's Collective Help 153
  SQ 5 154
   On the Other Side's Shifting Effort 154
  SQ 6 155
   On Effects of Death by War 155
  SQ 7 156

    On 19th Century Golden Age 156

  SQ 8 157
    On others impeding human progress 157

Additional BICS Questions 2 161
  AQ 1 161
    On the gap between tech and spiritual evolution 161

  AQ 2 161
    On spiritual help during the last 170 years 161

  AQ 3 162
    On sabotaging spirits 162

  AQ 4 162
    On forbidden information 162

  AQ 5 163
    On beneficial information 163

  AQ 6 164
    On reincarnation 164

  AQ 7 165
    On alien and discarnate human relationship 165

  AQ 8 165
    On individual and collective spiritual help 165

  AQ 9 166
    On evidential validation 166

Limitations of the BICS Study 173
  Unsubstantiated assumptions 174
  BICS Questions Ignored NDE Research 175
  NDEs and the Relativity of Time 176
  Limitations of The BICS Questions 177

The Brain as an Antenna 179

The World as a Spiritual School 183

  A.- Five Major Conclusions 183
  B.- The Present State of Humankind 184
  C.- Earth is a School 186
Consciousness and the Informational Universe 191
Considerations 197
Final Conclusions by Melvin Morse, MD 199
About the Authors 203

Foreword

Raymond Moody, MD, Ph.D.

Almost 50 years ago, I published *Life After Life*, a groundbreaking work that revealed the extraordinary nature of near-death experiences. It documented that at the end of life comes a new beginning, a sense of leaving the physical body and entering into a loving, brilliant light, indeed often becoming that light. More recently, I published Proof of Life After Life, Seven Reasons to Believe in the Afterlife, which is the culmination of over 50 years of my studies on what happens to us when we die.

Dozens of scientific papers have now documented what so many patients had told me, that the near-death experience is not only real, but it is the dying experience: we will all have one when we die. Dr. Melvin Morse's studies of the near-death experiences of children, published in the American Medical Association's Pediatric Journal, are perhaps the most compelling of these studies. These experiences demonstrate that we do not die but pass to another dimension of life, and yet we can still communicate with those who are living, albeit near death. Death itself is apparently just a body problem.

Dr. Morse and his colleagues at the Institute for the Scientific Study of Consciousness (ISSC) have taken the next step: they have convincingly demonstrated that the living can communicate with those disincarnated spirits in an all-informational domain often referred to as The Other Side. Although not currently accepted by the medical establishment as "real," this finding comes as no surprise to those of us who have studied near-death experiences. One of the most powerful aspects of the near-death experience is precisely what Dr. Morse and his colleagues describe:

communicating with conscious entities during the time that the experiencer's body is clinically dead. They return, reporting that they have communicated with dead relatives and often a loving, conscious "God." Dozens of cases have documented that these communications from conscious entities, which exist independently of our earthly existence, contain information that the experiencer would have no way of otherwise knowing except by communicating with those entities.

Dr. Morse told me of one compelling experience which illustrates this point. A law enforcement agent in Delaware told him of his near-death experience, which occurred while he was riding his motorcycle. He survived a horrendous accident that involved the motorcycle cartwheeling over and over as it skidded on a roadway made slick by a sudden thunderstorm. He was in a coma for several days yet miraculously made a full recovery.

He told Dr. Morse that he was not frightened during the experience, as he was comforted by his father, who had previously died. His father reassured him that he would be all right and learn from this experience. He protested to his father, asking him, "How can I believe this is real?" His father told him to ask his mother to look in a drainpipe in their home to find something he lost years ago. After he recovered, he went to visit his mother and told her that he had met his father when he went to heaven during his motorcycle accident. She expressed total disbelief, initially telling him it must have been some crazy dream until they looked in the drainpipe and found his wedding ring, which he had lost thirty years prior.

Again and again, the information that those who have had near-death experiences receive from the spirits of departed loved ones, guardian angels, and an all-knowing, unconditionally loving light is validated by subsequent events.

The scientists at ISSC have taken near-death research to the next level; they have worked with mediums, people who are living but not near death who have the talent and skill to contact disincarnate entities to obtain information that can be verified in this reality. ISSC scientists created a protocol known as "Spiritual Sight" that presents known aspects of this reality, such as people, places, or things, coded as numbers to conceal their identification, which the viewer (the person working the protocol) or medium is expected to describe in unmistakable detail. This protocol is based on the highly successful military-controlled remote viewing program developed at Stanford Research Institute by physicist Hal Puthoff, among others.

I have interviewed numerous people who have had near-death experiences who return to tell us that they entered into a domain in which they knew everything there is to know. Dr. Morse and ISSC have built on this, saying, "Okay, if you are in contact with a domain of all knowledge, then what is the target associated with this nine-digit number? "After all, that is a piece of information, yet it can be verified to ascertain if the viewer is genuinely in contact with such a domain. An informational domain that physicists such as John Wheeler tell us is the universe's very nature.

Fifty years ago, I coined the term "near-death experience," which resulted in a revolution in the way we perceive death. Fifty years later, I am proud to be a member of the ISSC team, which has now shown that we survive death and communicate with conscious discarnate entities while still alive. These entities have an urgent message for humankind, one that we can trust as accurate, not the product of the imaginations of the mediums. This urgent message should be shared with all of humanity; our future depends on it.

Foreword

Col (R) John B. Alexander, Ph.D.

This book is a report of a snapshot in time responding to four questions posited by the Bigelow Institute of Consciousness Studies (BICS). This specific report was created in response to an announcement by BICS that it was accepting applications for grants on research into postmortem communications. It is worth noting that hundreds of applications were submitted from all over the world. Of those, six were accepted, including only three from the United States and three from foreign countries. That alone speaks to the intense scrutiny that was applied and just how competitive the application process was.

The following statement, taken from the BICS website on 14 June 2024, is a capstone document encompassing all of the studies supported by BICS during the 2023-2024 cycle. It illustrates the importance of this study and ISSC's priceless contribution.

"BICS Challenge Program

"Has the Spirit World Failed Humanity?

"In 2023, BICS issued a ground-breaking challenge to the Spirit World. Sixty-seven hand-picked, certified mediums, comprising six teams in three countries, were funded $390,000 over nine months to connect with the afterlife to answer the question:"

"Has the Spirit World failed to enhance human spirituality on Earth since 1857 as evidenced by the dramatic rise in wars, violence and uncontrolled technology at the expense of human spirituality?"

The project director, Dr. Melvin Morse, brought to the study a lengthy history of research into near-death studies (NDEs). He also embodied original thinking, integrating seemingly disparate subjects and elucidating their fascinating connections.

Experienced, Dr. Morse first rose to prominence in the NDE field with his groundbreaking book *Closer to the Light: Learning from the Near-Death Experiences of Children*. As a critical care pediatrician at Seattle's Children's Hospital, what he brought to the topic were reports from children, most of whom had not been exposed to the burgeoning entertainment recounting and popularization of accounts of adults reporting fantastic encounters when close to death. Their age limited the probability that their NDE reports were simply recantations taken from television programs or other media events.

Entering the field skeptically, his first inclination was to assume that the extraordinary reports were mostly the product of some drug introduced during resuscitation or in the treatment of the child. Confronted with hard evidence that drug-induced psychosis could be ruled out, meticulously, he gathered material that pointed to the physical reality of the NDEs that were being reported. To that end, years before the book's publication, he authored his study results in the peer-reviewed *American Journal of Disease in Children*.

Dr. Morse's innovative research

Among the innovations Dr. Morse brought to the field was the integration of remote viewing as a mechanism for research into other psi-related phenomena—including NDEs and now postmortem communication. By employing what is known as coordinate remote viewing (CRV), the process removes any participants' direct knowledge of the intended target. In this case, the actual questions were replaced with random numbers that had become formally associated with that question via intention.

Innovatively, Dr. Morse was one of the first researchers to combine CRV with NDEs to reduce the investigators' intentional or unintentional leading. He first reported this technique at the International Remote Viewing Association (IRVA) conference in Las Vegas. He is an excellent example of how disparate approaches can be combined to enhance the results.

The present book provides readers with the information gleaned by the subset of mediums engaged by Dr. Morse and the ISSC organization. The reader will determine the validity or importance they ascribe to that information.

The audience is encouraged to read this study's general discussion and conclusions, as there is much helpful information. As stated in Chapter VI's beginning, " ....there seems to be solid evidence of true communication between humans and TOS (The Other Side), something that science has not accepted to this date." It is too soon to tell what impact these studies will have on the scientific community at large. It is clearly the audience to which such studies should be targeted.

The current changing scientific paradigm

The works of Thomas Kuhn are being widely discussed both here and in other survival of consciousness-related fora. Decades ago, Kuhn began writing about the necessity for a paradigm shift in thinking about the nature of consciousness. His book, *The Structure of Scientific Revolutions*, is being considered more frequently. In general, scientists have been indoctrinated in a materialist-dominated world, with consciousness being something that was generated in the human brain. As far back as the late 1800s, scientists such as Max Planck, a Nobel Prize-winning German physicist, posited that consciousness was fundamental and the physical (Real World) arose from consciousness. He also noted that "Science advances one funeral at a time." With studies such as conducted by the ISSC we hope to increase the speed of acceptance – and based on scientific data.

Please read this book, and though it has limitations, understand that it brings to light much practical information and adds to the total body of knowledge of consciousness studies.

John B. Alexander, Ph.D.

Las Vegas, NV

About the Study

Melvin L. Morse, MD

"Wow, I am flying through the air. This is amazing. This is fun!"

I had just given a random string of numbers to a medium I was interviewing to be part of the Bigelow Consciousness Institute Challenge Grant on mediumship. These numbers were assigned to a picture of Robbie Knievel jumping the Grand Canyon. But she had no way of knowing that. The only information I gave her were those nine numbers I had previously assigned to Robbie Knievel's daring feat. She said to me: "The wind is in my face. This is scary but thrilling." Then, an odd look came over her face. She said, "You know, I love to ride motorcycles. Somehow, this reminds me of riding a motorcycle, but that doesn't make any sense because I am flying, not riding."

Our team, The Institute for the Scientific Study of Consciousness, was tasked by the Bigelow Institute with interviewing 19 mediums to do a study that potentially has enormous importance for humanity. The mediums were to contact a discarnate entity and ask that entity four questions about the spiritual state of humanity, addressing the issue of why the world seems to be consumed by violence and hatred. Even the major religions are at war with each other, with Hindus, Christians, Muslims, and Jews all actively killing each other, often convinced that they are right and that they alone worship the only true God. This religious chaos occurs during great social and political unrest throughout the world. The Bigelow Institute wants to understand the spiritual world's take on what is happening. Has the spiritual world failed humanity, allowing us to plummet into a situation where human self-extinction is a real possibility? Or were imperfect humans or perhaps evil spirits to blame?

Most importantly, what can be done about it from a spiritual point of view? We often forget that spiritual understandings create enormous changes in how humans think, both positively and negatively. For example, spiritual communications with sages and enlightened individuals in the past made the world's great religions, which have been agents of profound changes in how we relate to each other. The Bigelow Institute wants to learn if the spirit world has a message for us now that could similarly transform the world.

As a scientist, I know the scientific mainstream does not accept mediumship. Yet I also understand that our current understanding of the universe is comprised of information embedded in the vast electromagnetic field in which we are all enmeshed. If we are all interconnected by one universal field of consciousness, then in theory, we should be able to access that information even though it is not accessible to our mind/brain through our ordinary senses. As Michael Shermer wrote in Scientific American, we are all complex clusters of information; what he terms information, representing the memories, personality, and sense of self that is a human, could be considered a soul in religious terms. Since this cluster of information that is a human is embedded in the timeless spaceless electromagnetic energy field that is reality, our souls, in theory, are eternal from a scientific perspective.

The most prominent scientists of our time, including Robert Lanza, who altered the genetics of a chicken at age 13, which caught the attention of researchers at Harvard Medical School, have proposed exactly that: that reality is based on a universal field of consciousness, which is the substrate of all that we perceive as real. Dr. Lanza, arguably the world's most brilliant scientist, has proposed that everything we experience, including Newtonian physics and quantum physics, is a system created by our consciousness. Even space and time are tools our minds use to assemble information from the universe. Ultimate reality is without time or space; those are human creations necessary to interact with each other and essential to navigating this mutually shared reality.

So, nothing in modern science contradicts the concept of mediumship, meaning that an individual's consciousness can interact with a universal consciousness or other individual consciousnesses, which can be seen as living or dead from our point of view. Indeed, mediumship does not fit into the now-discredited materialistic scientific paradigm in which the individual brain creates consciousness. Materialism, which reigned supreme in the 19th and much of the 20th century, is now so discredited that there is no universally accepted definition of matter in the scientific community. We are currently in a paradigm shift; studies such as this one will be one of many scientific studies that will result in a new paradigm. Recent scientific evidence indicates that the brain acts as an antenna or perhaps is a tool consciousness uses to interact with other humans in this particular realm of reality.

Why We Presented The Bics Questions As Numbers

Although mediumship is not in conflict with modern scientific models of reality, it is not accepted by the scientific community. Scientists and mediums have had an ugly relationship for over 150 years, which has only resulted in confusion. In the nineteenth century, several prominent scientists took a keen interest in studying mediumship despite the prevailing skepticism of the time. Notable figures included chemist Robert Hare, physicist William Crookes, and evolutionary biologist Alfred Russel Wallace1. These scientists conducted various experiments to investigate the claims of mediums and the possibility of communicating with spirits. Unscrupulous mediums often duped them, and there were many scandals of con artists posing as mediums who fooled scientists and the general public. This has led to a general rejection of mediumship because it has previously been hard to differentiate a proper medium from a con artist. Furthermore, the various scientific studies of mediumship are often poorly designed and flawed.

In a recent comprehensive literature review of scientific evaluations of mediumship, a Brazilian group of scientists and physicians who are also mediums said that there was no overwhelming scientific evidence of mediumship, primarily because of lax attention to protocols and poorly designed studies. Mediums wrote this paper! So they knew mediumship was genuine as they practiced it, yet they also recognized that prior research had not been convincing. They called for truly blinded studies of mediumship.

We answered their challenge by devising a revolutionary means of blinding mediums to the tasks we were giving them. We coded each of the four BICS questions as a distinct nine-digit number. This way, the medium would have no way of knowing what the question was. They could only answer the question by contacting a discarnate entity privy to the comprehensive informational universe that physicists such as John Wheeler stated is reality. Children who have had near-death experiences and were still conscious even though they were clinically dead report that they had "all the knowledge" during the time they were out of their bodies. So, we have clinical observations that precisely match what theoretical physicists describe as ultimate reality. Or, as one child said of the universal informational universe, "It was real. It was realer than real". So, it is reasonable to speculate that mediums can contact discarnate entities with access to this universal informational source.

One piece of information they would have access to is the question we have assigned to the specific number. The details of which numbers corresponded to which questions were a closely guarded secret even within the ISSC team. This ensured that the mediums could only answer the questions by actually contacting a discarnate entity. And that is precisely what happened in our study. For example, one medium contacted a discarnate entity and said," I have questions for you, but I don't know what they are." The entity replied, "But we do."

We Set The Standards For Mediumship

The BICS project is of urgent interest to humanity. We were responsible for ensuring that our mediums were of the highest caliber and character so that whatever messages they obtained from The Other Side could be trusted.

We expected our mediums to 1) demonstrate proficiency in an advanced form of the elite military-controlled remote viewing protocol and 2) demonstrate the ability to alter a stream of electrons with their minds. By doing this, we knew we were working with mediums with the highest skill levels and abilities.

ISSC had previously developed a scientific protocol called Spiritual Sight, based on military-grade controlled remote viewing protocols. We consulted with the foremost remote viewers, including Lyn Buchanan, featured in Men Who Stare at Goats, and Professor Courtney Brown of Emory University.

The military-controlled remote viewing protocol has had numerous successes over the years, including assisting in the capture of Saddam Hussein, locating downed military aircraft, and describing the location and details of the secret Soviet research and development site known as Sugar Grove. The program is highly classified. However, insiders have told me that several Presidents have awarded medals to remote viewers recognizing their contributions to our nation's security.

ISSC team members have been extensively trained in the military-controlled remote viewing program and subsequently developed Spiritual Sight, a form of remote viewing useful for civilian purposes. Lyn Buchanan termed it "applied remote viewing" as it has spiritual healing and mediumship applications.

The Spiritual Sight protocol uses numbers to identify the session's task or target, decrease mental noise, and prevent the viewer from grafting their preconceptions onto the information-gathering session.

This is why I tested the medium's ability to access information from a universal source by giving her a specific number, 123456789, corresponding to Robbie Knievel's jump from the Grand Canyon on a motorcycle. This number was chosen to be unique and unrelated to any preconceived notions or personal experiences, thereby ensuring that the information accessed was not influenced by the medium's own thoughts or memories.

This particular medium, Deb Torres, was a psychic who worked for the FBI, helping to solve cases involving missing persons and cold cases. In her 27-year career with the FBI, she had 154 successful cases. So, we were not surprised that she could effortlessly identify the random number corresponding to Robbie Knievel's daredevil stunt.

All the mediums selected for our study demonstrated proficiency in Spiritual Sight.

Our second criterion for selecting them as one of the challenge grant mediums was that they had to demonstrate that they could alter the flow of a stream of electrons with their minds. We used a true random number generator developed by the Department of Engineering at Princeton University. These random number generators are essential for encrypting information for the banking industry, among other uses. However, physicists for the Boeing Corporation and Engineers at Princeton discovered that the human mind could alter the flow of electrons in the devices in certain altered states of consciousness. Even skeptics such as Carl Sagan recognized this was a natural human ability.

The ability to alter the flow of electrons with one's mind is a marker for the altered state of consciousness necessary for mediumship. Prior published scientific studies by ISSC have documented that when military-controlled remote viewers successfully accessed information from a remote source, they also altered the flow of electrons in the random number generators. Similarly, when Reiki healers successfully improved a patient's clinical care, they likewise changed the flow of electrons in the devices. When deep in prayer, Carmelite Nuns can also change the flow of electrons in these devices.

Mediums were rigorously selected for our study based on their ability to alter the flow of electrons in a true random number generator for at least 10 minutes in a 30-minute session, a criterion established by Professor Mario Beauregard of the University of Montreal. This stringent selection process ensured the credibility of our findings.

Our revolutionary study protocol vetted the mediums by ensuring they could access information from the universal informational universe. This theoretical construct represents a collective repository of all knowledge and experiences. This was demonstrated by retrieving that information after being given a nine-digit number. They also had to have the psychic ability to alter a random stream of electrons with their minds.

Evaluation of the Mediums

José Miguel Gaona, MD

Science has always been afraid to address the study of those issues that apparently could not be measured. However, paradoxically, many of the most critical issues for human beings are not measurable, among which are emotions, some of which are among the most valued, such as love for a partner or children or loyalty. Still, there are also others that have been endorsed by millions of people and that are found within the spiritual facet by millions of people over millennia. Mental abilities such as premonitions, telepathy, or remote viewing are all of them framed within the spiritual realm.

Prejudices against mediums often arise from misconceptions and cultural biases. Many perceive mediums as mystical, dismissing their spiritual practices as outdated or irrational. Such prejudices overlook the deep cultural significance and healing traditions embedded within rituals. By stereotyping mediums, individuals may overlook valuable insights into spiritual connection with other realms. Challenging these prejudices involves acknowledging the rich diversity of spiritual practices worldwide and recognizing the potential benefits of psychological wisdom in fostering personal growth and healing.

However, in our study group, we wanted to measure certain issues typical of people who live in the spiritual world, whether they are called priests, shamans, or mediums. To do this, we launched a Cartesian study, through which we wanted to know the psychological personality profile of those individuals who seemed to present special powers. Despite applying psychometric measurement methods, we have not used any science to achieve psychological or psychiatric diagnoses but rather personality profiling.

In the following pages, we show a tiny part of our data and hold data interrelations for future publications.

Filiation data

First of all, we were interested in the filtration data of those who belong to the study—a question as essential as knowing your sex, age, number of children, and other types of questions that we found relevant. It has caught our attention that the average profile of the participants is at a mature age (44 years on average). It is also striking that practically two-thirds of them are female (62.5%), and just over half do not have a partner (53.3%).

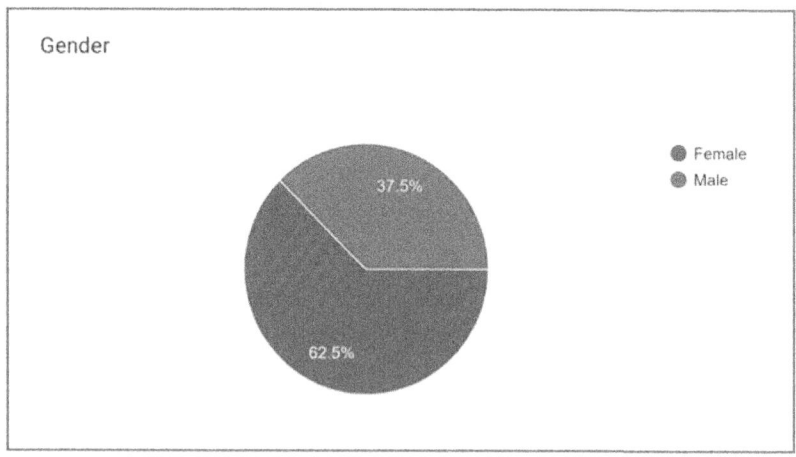

It is striking that the average age at which they began to perceive their powers was about 16.3 years, with the same being present for 43.8%. In this same order of things, almost one in four (25%) felt fear.

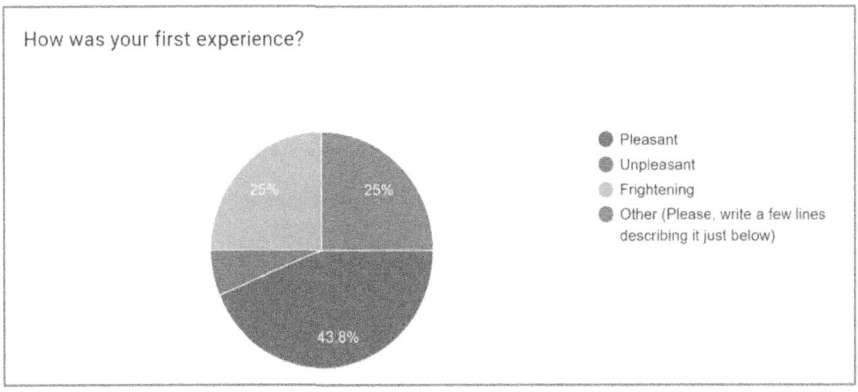

It is also striking that a large majority (87.5%) of this age range have perceived that their powers have increased with age. From the family point of view, a large part of the participants (81.3%) had relatives who also exhibited the same qualities, which leads us to think that there could be systemic cultural factors within that same structure or, venturing the hypothesis, issues of a neurological type that had an impact on remote vision.

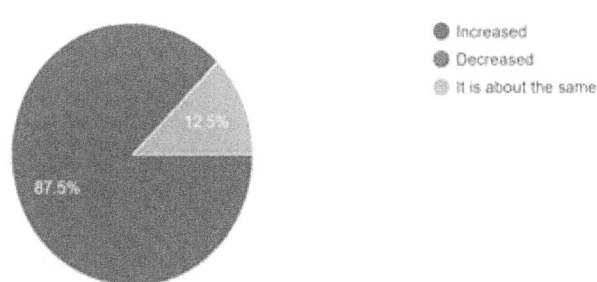

It is also essential to emphasize that mediums usually participate in three senses: hearing (56.3%), touch (56.3%), and vision, which is reached by 50% of them.

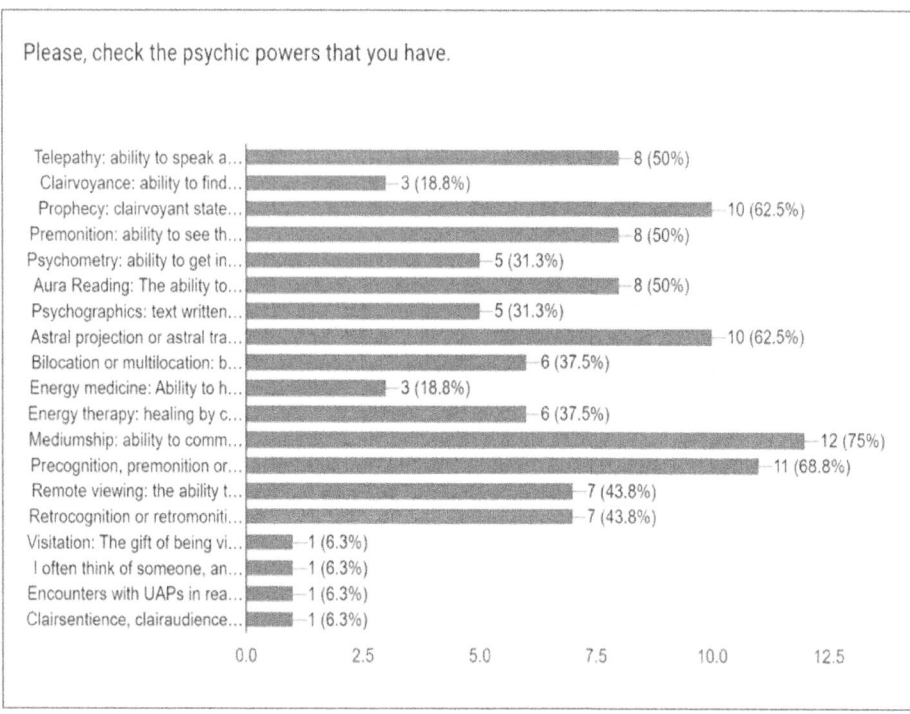

In addition to the above, we have studied other types of abilities, such as telepathy, premonition, bilocation, encounters with disembodied beings, out-of-body Experiences, and a long list of others, which we will explain in our final report.

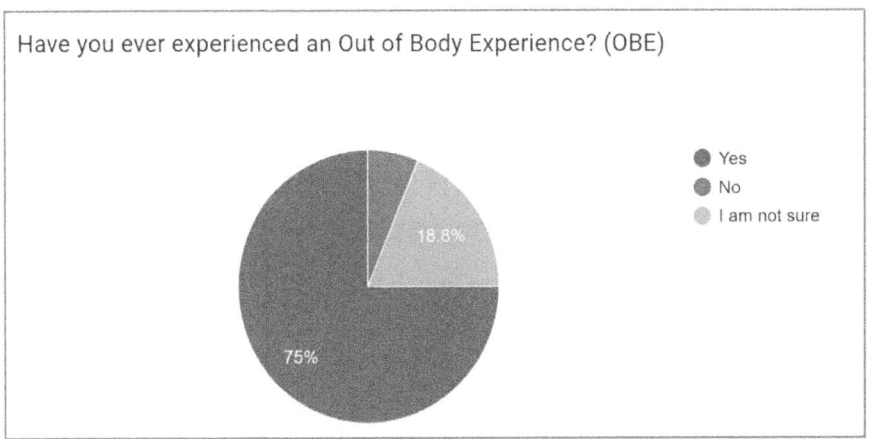

Psychological profile

Secondly, we wanted to explore the psychological profile more deeply through the Millon Multiaxial Clinical Inventory-IV (MCMI-IV).

The Millon Clinical Multiaxial Inventory-IV (MCMI-IV) is a self-report instrument designed to assess the personality and psychopathology of adults receiving psychological or psychiatric care or treatment.

The MCMI-IV has a series of characteristics that distinguish it from other personality inventories:

- Scales based on the prestigious evolutionary theory of personality of Dr. Theodore Millon.
- Assessment of a wide range of relevant domains, consistent with the personality disorders included in the DSM-5 and ICD-10 classifications and the most relevant clinical syndromes.
- Facilitates the identification of deep and widespread clinical problems.
- Your therapeutic approach provides the basis for making effective treatment decisions.

- Use of base rates that guarantee that the frequency of diagnoses and personality patterns obtained are representative of the underlying prevalences in the clinical population.

- Brevity and understandable language that reduces application time and minimizes the subject's effort and fatigue.

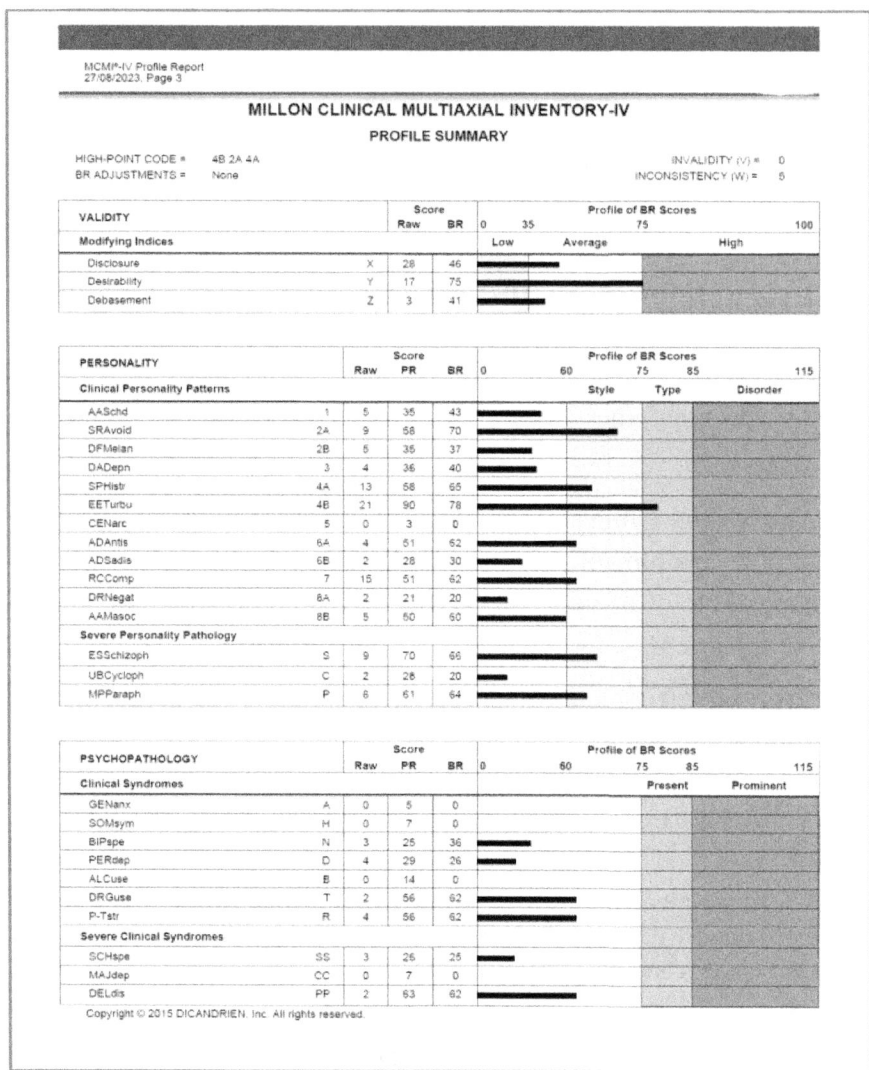

(Millon Inventory of one of the mediums. Names have been erased)

The findings have been extremely interesting and constitute a unique opportunity worldwide to study a profile as defined as that of mediums, especially to study their personality patterns. It is striking that, although some of them expressed having had a psychiatric history (45%) during the evaluation, their profiles were within normality.

Factors related to dissociation

In addition to the above, and thirdly, we will consider the field experience in which we observed apparent dissociative states. In those who make up the study, we wanted to apply a scale, such as the Steinberg Inventory, that could measure this state, which is nothing more than a disconnection between a person's mind and the reality of the present moment. Something important that we must highlight is that this disconnection can occur both externally and internally. Even easier, we can disconnect from what is happening outside of us but also from our mental activity (thoughts, emotions, sensations).

Sometimes, we dissociate as a protection system for our mind. This may initially be a positive thing, but the problem will arise later since while we are dissociated, we cannot integrate and manage anything that happens. This implies that we will have an unmanaged matter which will subsequently emerge during our lives. We have noticed this on other occasions during fieldwork. Dissociation appears to occur during the medium's trance. At that moment, the person seems to abandon the physical world and immerses himself in another reality, where he can obtain information that could not be obtained under another psychological situation. In fact, the professionals who have participated in the different remote viewing sessions have been able to appreciate situations, attitudes, and behaviors compatible with altered states of consciousness, similar to those that this researcher has noticed in shamanic profiles.

Allan Kardec's 1857 Study

AJ Parr

Allan Kardec, born Hippolyte Léon Denizard Rivail, is renowned as the founder of Spiritism. This philosophical and spiritual movement explores the nature of spirits and their interactions with the physical world. One of Kardec's most significant contributions to this field is "The Spirits' Book," published in 1857. This groundbreaking work is not just a collection of spiritual teachings; it results from a meticulous and methodical spiritual experiment that Kardec conducted to investigate the consistency of spirit communications and the state of humanity at the time.

Kardec approached his research with the rigor and objectivity of a scientific researcher. He recognized the need for a systematic method to evaluate the information received from spirits. This led him to design an experiment to ensure the reliability and coherence of spiritual messages.

Kardec collaborated with various mediums in different places, which helped eliminate any biases that might arise from a single source. He could also cross-verify the information received from different spirits by working with multiple mediums.

Kardec prepared a comprehensive list of questions covering a wide range of topics related to the nature of spirits, the afterlife, morality, and the universe. These were carefully crafted to probe deeply into the spiritual knowledge and perspectives of the spirits.

This rigorous scientific methodology allowed Kardec to treat spiritual communication with unprecedented scrutiny and seriousness, solidifying Spiritism's credibility as a philosophical and spiritual doctrine.

Consulting Multiple Spirits

Kardec's questions were posed to different spirits through various mediums. He did not rely on the responses of a single spirit; instead, he sought answers from multiple spirits across different sessions. This approach was akin to collecting data from various sources to ensure a robust and reliable set of responses. One of the critical aspects of Kardec's methodology was the comparison of responses. He meticulously analyzed the answers given by different spirits to the same questions, looking for consistency and coherence. Kardec believed that if the spirits were genuine and their messages were truthful, there would be a significant degree of agreement among their responses.

After gathering and analyzing the responses, Kardec compiled consistent and coherent answers into the 1857 book, "The Spirits' Book." Its pages are structured in a question-and-answer format, providing a comprehensive overview of the spirits' teachings and insights.

In total, "The Spirits' Book" was compiled with 501 questions and answers in its first edition. The second edition expanded to 1,018 questions, and the final edition included 1,019 questions, reflecting the evolving nature of Spiritist teachings. Kardec's meticulous approach and dedication to primary sources ensured that the answers were presented verbatim, with minimal editorialization, providing a clear and authentic representation of the spirits' messages.

Kardec's role was not merely that of a compiler; he critically assessed the information, ensuring it aligned with rational and moral principles.

The Science Behind Kardec's Research

Kardec's approach to spirit communication was revolutionary because it introduced a scientific spirit to studying spiritual phenomena. He treated the process with the same meticulous care and skepticism that a scientist would apply to a research project. Kardec aimed to establish Spiritism as a credible and rational field of study by seeking corroboration and consistency.

"The Spirits' Book" remains a cornerstone of Spiritism, revered for its systematic approach and the depth of its insights. Kardec's innovative experiment demonstrated that spiritual inquiry could be pursued with scientific rigor, paving the way for future studies in the field.

Even to this day, Kardec's revolutionary research work continues to inspire those who seek to understand the spiritual dimensions of existence through a balanced and methodical lens.

Kardec's Main Conclusions

These are some of the critical conclusions from Kardec's research, which, as we shall see, were also reflected in the responses from the nineteen mediums interviewed by ISSC during the BICS Challenge:

On the Nature of Spirits

Spirits are the intelligent beings of creation, distinct from the human soul but capable of influencing the material world and the lives of individuals. They are the principal beings of the universe, with humans being temporary incarnations of these spirits.

On Reincarnation

Spirits undergo a process of reincarnation, living multiple lives across different bodies to evolve and progress. Each new life offers moral and intellectual advancement opportunities, contributing to the spirit's journey toward perfection.

On Earth as a School

Life on Earth serves as a school for spirits, where they face challenges and experiences that help them grow spiritually.

On the Role of Tribulations

The trials and tribulations encountered are seen as lessons designed to foster development and self-improvement.

On Moral Progress:

Moral development is central to spiritual progress. Good deeds, ethical behavior, and the practice of virtues like charity, humility, and compassion are essential for the elevation of the spirit.

On Cause and Effect:

The universe operates under the law of cause and effect (karma), where every action has consequences. This law ensures that justice prevails and individuals are accountable for their actions across lifetimes.

On Communication with Spirits:

Spirits can communicate with the living through mediums, providing insights, guidance, and knowledge from the spiritual realm.

On Free Will

Free will is a fundamental aspect of the human experience. Spirits have the freedom to make choices, and their moral and spiritual progress depends on using this free will to make ethical decisions.

On Spiritual Hierarchy

Spirits exist at various levels of development, forming a hierarchy based on their moral and intellectual advancement. Lower spirits are more materialistic and selfish, while higher spirits are more enlightened and virtuous. All spirits are destined to progress toward higher states of being.

In sum, Allan Kardec's creation of "The Spirits' Book" was a groundbreaking experiment that blended scientific methodology with spiritual inquiry. By consulting multiple mediums and spirits, formulating precise questions, and analyzing responses for consistency, Kardec established a robust framework for understanding the spirit world. This made a lasting impact on the study of spirituality and set the ground for future research, including the BICS challenge.

BICS Challenge Final Report

An Investigation into the Current Status of the Spiritual Progress of Humanity, as Ascertained by Interviewing 19 Mediums

"If there be a doctrine that should win over the most incredulous by its charm and its beauty, it is that of the existence of spirit-protectors or guardian angels. To think that you always have near you beings who are superior to you and who are always beside you to counsel you, to sustain you, to aid you in climbing the steep ascent of self-improvement, whose friendship is truer and more devoted than the most intimate union that you can contract upon the earth-is not such an idea most consoling?"

Allan Kardec The Spirits Book (Question 495)

I.- Abstract

Upside Down on The Roller Coaster:
An Urgent Message for Humanity

A scientific team comprising a neuroscientist, forensic psychiatrist, attorney, and a science-trained medium embarked on a groundbreaking journey. They interviewed 19 mediums, each with unique abilities, to delve into the urgent questions about humanity's spiritual development. These questions, formulated by the Bigelow Institute for Consciousness Studies (BICS), challenged the spiritual world to assess humanity's spiritual progress since the time of Allan Kardec (1857). The questions explore whether humans have progressed spiritually in the past 167-plus years, and if not, who is to blame? Has the spirit world failed humanity, or have humans failed, either by themselves, sabotage, or impediments by corrupted spirits and earthbound entities? One underlying concern is whether humanity's technology has outstripped its spiritual development, placing itself at risk of extinction.

The mediums contacted the highest spiritual entities, including The I AM, St. James, and Allan Kardec, to address these questions.

The scientists took a revolutionary approach to interviewing mediums by encoding the questions as numbers and then presenting the numbers to the mediums as questions. The mediums demonstrated proficiency at Spiritual Sight, an advanced form of the US Military Intelligence Services remote viewing protocol. Additionally, they had to demonstrate the ability to shift the flow of electrons in a transistor with their minds. An attorney observed the interviews and a forensic psychiatrist assessed the mediums.

The findings revealed that although humans have failed to make significant progress in the past 167-plus years, failure is an essential component of progress. The spirits acknowledged that spiritual progress is often a roller coaster, as wars and catastrophes are often necessary learning experiences, yet humanity is currently "upside down on the roller coaster."

The spirit world firmly states and presents evidence that humankind is solely to blame for the current situation. They have consistently provided spiritual guidance, such as the Ten Commandments. They sent prophets, religious leaders, and enlightened individuals such as Martin Luther King Jr. On a personal level, they inspire, nudge, cajole, and manipulate humans to achieve spiritual progress daily. They cheer humanity on and are partners in their spiritual evolution.

The entities contacted provided numerous specific examples of their interventions, from inspiring the scientific advancements of the Enlightenment to creating an Ice Age to move humans around the globe. They stated that they inspired the technology of the Iron Age to make the cultural conditions that directly led to the Axial Age, the birth of the great religions.

However, they typically play the "hands-off" role of parents watching their child learn to walk. Although repeated failure is part of the process, parents will intervene when safety is an issue. As one entity said while showing an image of two women driving a car purposely off a cliff: "That is what free will can bring you."

They explained that Earth is a learning center or spiritual school in which benevolent entities expertly and subtly guide human existence. Death is one of the greatest agents in promoting spiritual development, which permits the soul to rest and reflect on what it learned.

This understanding of reality challenges prevailing attitudes towards life and death, advocates for a reassessment of humanity's interaction with the unseen, and emphasizes the importance of deep reflection on how spiritual forces influence human beings. Death is not to be feared—far from it. It is an essential mechanism for spiritual growth and often the only time spent reflecting on what has been learned spiritually.

However, humans cannot learn from catastrophic failure. This is why the spirit world influenced BICS to ask these questions and share this urgent message with humanity.

II.- Introduction

BICS funded teams of scientists to present to mediums four questions concerning the current status of humanity's spiritual progress, with specific emphasis on the time period since the publication of Allan Kardec's The Spirit World in 1857. (Kardec 2017) They are:

1. "Since 1857, has the Other Side failed and Mankind failed to achieve good progress in securing human spirituality? If so, are bad spirits and bad humans winning?

2. Explain to people on Earth why the Other Side has not failed in fostering spiritual evolution.

3. What difference has the Other Side made in the past 166 years in influencing humans to accelerate their spiritual progress?

4. To what extent have earthbound spirits since 1857 impeded, sabotaged, or distorted the progress of human spiritual evolution?

Who is ISSC?

The Institute for the Scientific Study of Consciousness was founded by Charles Tart, PhD, in 1979. Its associates include Dr. Jose Miguel Gaona, MD, Ph.D., Isabelle Chauffeton Saavedra, Lance Williams Beem, MA, Melvin L Morse, MD, and AJ Parr.

They were chosen to do this work because of their scientific rigor and intellectual agnosticism about the answers presented by the mediums. Their expertise is in study design and maintaining the integrity of the process so that they can be confident that these answers indeed came from the universe and are not a product of the mediums' imagination. All answers are faithfully presented in this text; they did not filter or cherry-pick the data in any way.

Dr. Morse, a neuroscientist and former Professor of Pediatrics at the University of Washington, has been repeatedly recognized by his peers as one of America's Best Doctors. (Naifeh 1997)(Fred Hutchison CRC 2002). While initially studying children's cancer treatment protocols and their effects on the brain. (Morse 1985)(Morse 1986), as a Pediatric Intensivist, published the first prospective study of near-death experiences (NDEs) in children who survived cardiac arrest at Seattle Children's Hospital. (Morse 1983, 1985, 1991, 1994)

Dr. Gaona is the medical director of the Neurosalus Institute, recognized by the Spanish Government as Spain's premiere neuropsychiatric treatment facility. A specialist in forensic neuropsychiatry, he has trained at Harvard in non-invasive brain techniques and served as a visiting Professor at Laurentian University, working with Michael Persinger, MD. He has a degree in Theology from Navarro University. He serves as a consultant responsible for the area of mental health in the Bosnian war for the NGO Doctors of the World. (Gaona 2015, 2022)

Isabelle Chauffeton Saavedra is the CEO of a successful event planning company whose clients include Microsoft, major healthcare industry corporations, and the first French astronaut to fly on the Discovery Shuttle. The author of three books on scientific mediumship, she pioneered the use of mediumship to contact a (living) comatose hospitalized patient to learn his quality-of-life needs. She was able to share with his family simple interventions such as playing him his favorite songs: simple interventions, to be sure, but ones that made a huge difference in his quality of life. (Chauffeton Saavedra I 2013, 2016)

AJ Parr is an internationally recognized spiritual journalist. He has spent three decades researching comparative religions, human consciousness, the origins of language, and near-death experiences, especially in children. His YouTube channel features interviews with near-death survivors, mediums, and virtually every major consciousness researcher. (Parr A 2014, 2020, 2023)

Lance Williams-Beem is the CEO of Beem Agro-Sciences Corp, a developer of natural plant extracts for use in agriculture. He is skilled in classic controlled remote viewing, as developed by the United States Central Intelligence Agency. He has published in the peer-reviewed scientific literature on spiritual healers' efforts to raise the white count of a severely neutropenic patient. (Morse M., Beem L. 2011)

Why is this Study Important?

Although the framework of the questions presented to the mediums involves four questions related to humanity's spiritual progress in the past 167-plus years, in fact, the answers address the greatest mysteries that have puzzled humanity since the dawn of time, such as: Is there a God or a spiritual dimension in charge of this world? If so, why is there so much evil, crime, wars, and calamities? Why does a loving God allow bad things to happen to good people? What are Earthbound spirits and ghosts, and what is their relationship to humanity's spiritual progress? Most importantly, it addresses the question of what "spiritual progress" is and what exactly the role of the spirit world is in fostering human spiritual progress.

III.- Experimental Design and Methods

The Mediums and Entities Contacted

Kardec stated that any investigation by mediums must proceed from two primary principles. 1) the mediums must be of the highest character. He advised caution in working with full-time professional mediums but did not rule out consulting them, but to be cautious in such circumstances. (2) The entities contacted must be of the highest spiritual level. These entities present intellectual manifestations and are far removed from earthly and material concerns.

The Selection of Mediums

The project started by recruiting only mediums of the highest character. They are all employed and are from all walks of life. They include an agent for the United States Federal Bureau of Investigation (FBI), a veterinarian, an author of two books on scientific mediumship, factory workers, college students, paranormal investigators, a health care executive for a non-profit corporation, social workers, a trainer of other mediums and employees of the United States Veterans Administration.

Their ability to demonstrate Spiritual Sight was assessed. Spiritual Sight (Morse M, Saavedra I, 2014) begins with the highly structured controlled remote viewing protocol used by the United States Military Intelligence Services. Dr. Morse is an acknowledged expert on controlled remote viewing, having received the prestigious Warcollier Award for Consciousness Research from the International Remote Viewers Association, the civilian face of the United States military intelligence remote viewers. (irva.org) Under the guidance of Lyn Buchanan, he developed an Applied Remote Viewing protocol applicable for mediumship and spiritual healing (Lyn Buchanan personal communication 2017 March). Dr. Morse and Ms. Chauffeton Saavedra then further adapted the protocol for this project.

Spiritual Sight involves retrieving information about an unknown target through non-ordinary means. A remote target, such as the Eiffel Tower, is given a nine-digit number as the psychic address for the information cluster corresponding to the Eiffel Tower. The number alone is given to the medium. They can retrieve information associated with the unknown site as they work the Spiritual Sight protocol. The team then compares their efforts to a picture of the actual sight. Their efforts are scored as a "direct hit," "site contact," (meaning some elements of the target are retrieved but not enough to make sense of the target), and "miss."

For example, one of the mediums was given a number that was associated with an older woman who had severe atrial fibrillation that required hospitalization.

She touched the woman's hand and spoke words of comfort to her. Upon discussing the case with the elderly woman after the session was over, she stated: "I was in my hospital room. I heard someone say "hello," but there was no one in the room. I felt something touch my arm and heard, 'Your daughter will be here soon.' No one seemed to be present. My daughter did arrive a few minutes later."

This shows that the medium can assess information through non-ordinary means and contact with a consciousness separate from their mind/brain. The woman's atrial fibrillation coincidentally resolved after the medium contacted her with Spiritual Sight.

Strategesian
3:17   813 298 231

[handwritten sketch of a figure with outstretched arms]

Target is biological. flesh colored white, repititious sound, medium, warm, hair, rough, old, a little afraid. Heart is weak, not working. Mom said to Carol "Be with me". She seems to be in a bed, hospital, frightened. She is either sleeping or resting. Your Mom is afraid she is dying. I had Carol crying for 5 min. She squeezed Carol's hand at 3:18, opened eyes at 3:37.

After being given the number 813298231, the medium worked the Spiritual Sight protocol. As can be seen above, she scored a direct hit. She gained information from the target: "The target is biological, flesh-colored, white, repetitious sound, warm, hair, rough, old, a little afraid. The heart is weak, not working." Once she and her monitor were sure she was at the intended cluster of information corresponding to the older woman, she interacted with the woman. In this case, the woman is still alive. However, the process is the same if the entity contacted is discarnate.

Finally, the team assessed the medium's ability to move a stream of electrons with their mind using the Psyleron random number generator the Princeton University Department of Engineering developed (psyleron.com)(Jahn R 2007). This quantum random number generator measures a chaotic stream of electrons to produce actual random numbers, which is essential for the banking industry to encrypt information. Dr. Morse has previously demonstrated that alterations in the electron stream by the mind of elite military remote viewers correlate with successful remote viewing efforts. (crvreg.org)

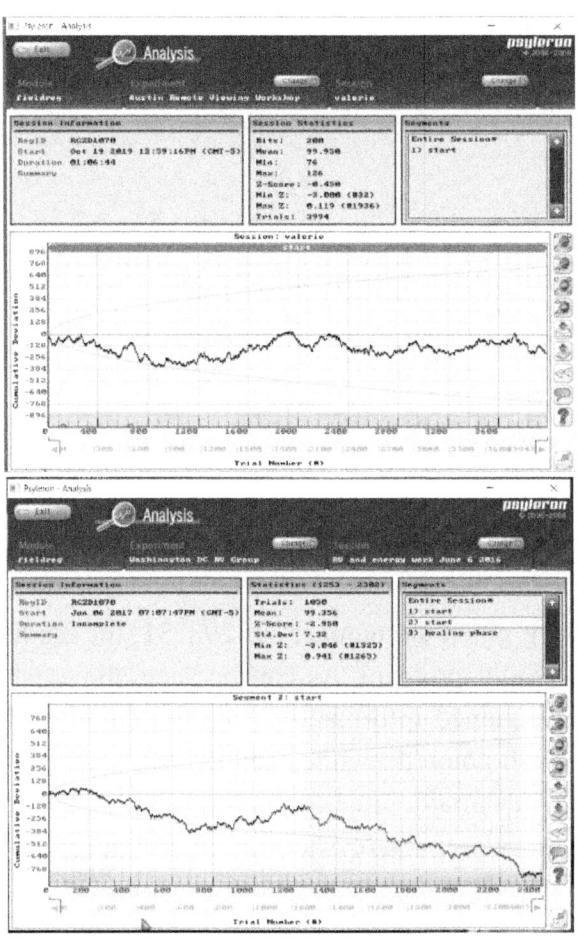

The graph on the top represents an unsuccessful controlled remote viewing effort by one of the elite military remote viewers. It is entirely random, as can be seen by the tracing staying close to the middle horizontal line, indicating randomness.

The graph on the bottom represents a successful healing effort using Spiritual Sight. The medium raised the oxygen concentration of a severely hypoxic woman with COPD, working entirely blinded from a nine-digit number that was assigned to the woman's medical condition. She caused the device to go nonrandom for over 10 minutes with a Z score of nearly 3 (highly statistically significant). At the same time, the woman's oxygen saturation level went from 86% to 94%.

The engineers who invented the device with a grant from the American Aerospace Company McDonald Douglas state that when mediums alter the electron flow of the device, this represents the ability to change the structure of reality itself (albeit in a very minor and limited way) (personal communication Herb Mertz PhD) This is based on the fact that this reality is made of quarks and electrons. (Cartwright J) The idea that the human mind can interact on a quantum level with electrons was first established by physicists working for the Boeing Corporation (Schmidt H 1969)(Radin D. 1989). Skeptic Carl Sagan mentioned it as worthy of further study. (Sagan C 1997 page 302)

The team expected the mediums to be able to alter the flow of electrons in the Psyleron device to a statistically significant degree for over 10 minutes per 30-minute session.

The Presentation of the Questions

The mediums were then presented with the BICS questions as numbers.

THE FOUR BICS QUESTIONS

QUESTION 1. 621055219:
QUESTION 2. 292846648
QUESTION 3. 879610310
QUESTION 4. 106261065

The mediums are all proficient in Spiritual Sight. Hence, they were confident they could obtain information from a target presented as a number even though, in this case, the target is an abstract concept representing the cluster of information pertinent to answering the question. Built into these numbers is the requirement that a discarnate entity be contacted to answer the questions properly.

14 Mediums were successful at this approach. However, the purpose of this study is to have mediums answer the questions, so if they could not answer the questions from numbers, they were asked to use their typical protocol for contacting entities to answer the questions. 5 Mediums took this approach.

Who are the Mediums?

There were 19 mediums selected for the project: 12 were from America's heartland, Fort Wayne, Indiana. This is one of America's most conservative and yet profoundly spiritual regions. Christian church attendance in the greater Fort Wayne area is over 50%, and it is one of America's top 10 Christian church-going areas. (barna.com)

Seven were from Charleston, South Carolina, a Southeastern port city that was the site of the earliest shots fired in the American Civil War. These are two very different areas in terms of culture and religious belief systems: a small midwestern town and one of the largest seaports in Southeast America.

<u>The Fort Wayne Mediums</u>: 8 of the mediums successfully answered the questions starting with a number instead of the written words.

Two of the mediums worked from full trance. They also answered the questions as numbers without any further prompting. The entities presented to the monitor directly from the medium.

Six of the mediums were what are termed "mental mediums." They are considered trance mediums, but they bilocate in that they can talk to the entity separately while talking to the monitor. The questions were presented as numbers until the entities contacted clearly indicated they knew the nature of the question. For example, one medium, on being given only the number for the first question, which has to do with whether or not the spirit world and humanity have failed to make good progress since the time of Allan Kardec, responded: "Progress can't be made unless there is a failure." At this point, specific questions were asked using words, not numbers.

Another medium, when given the number that corresponds to the same question, upon contacting an entity, stated, "I have questions for you, but I don't know what they are." (meaning she only knew the numbers) The entity replied, "But we do." The entity said that the spirit world had not failed humanity, nor has humanity failed, but that humans are on a roller coaster and are currently upside down!

In both cases, the mediums clearly contacted an entity familiar with the questions. Only after it was clear that the mediums contacted an entity who understood the question presented as a number were more specific follow-up questions presented.

This was necessary as the questions require greater specificity than the entities often answered when first presented with the number. The research design did not want platitudes and grand philosophical statements but actual specifics of how and when the spirit world has helped humanity to progress and precisely how it works.

Four of the mediums were what is termed "psychic mediums." This means they are not contacting the highest spiritual entities but instead communicate with spirit guides, personal guides, inner voices, and other lower-level entities, many of whom are earthbound spirits. They did not go into a trance but spoke from their deepest intuitions.

Three of these psychic mediums could not answer the questions in the form of numbers. So, the monitors, according to protocol, then posed the questions to whatever entities or guides were familiar to the mediums. They contributed significantly to the project by presenting fragments and more in-depth complementary pieces of the greater picture. It was found that their contributions fit precisely within the framework of the answers as provided by the core mediums.

<u>Charleston Mediums</u>: One medium was a full-trance medium that spoke directly in the voice of the entity contacted. Three mediums were mental mediums, and three were psychic mediums.

The four trance mediums were part of the core 12 trance mediums. They initially answered the questions as numbers, progressing to more detailed ones after it became clear that the entities contacted were familiar with them.

Three psychic mediums attempted to answer the questions as numbers without success and then proceeded to answer them as written using their individual protocols.

Medium 2003 illustrates the difficulties in determining whether a medium is psychic or trance. She describes herself as a psychic medium, meaning she contacts guides who are familiar to her. However, when the first question was presented in a blinded manner, she could not answer it, and the monitor then presented the questions as written. Yet she appeared to be in a trance when speaking with St. James. It seems that the unique nature of this project caused her to go into a trance, which is otherwise unusual for her, and the most valuable information came from her brief trance.

She has been designated a psychic medium, could not answer the questions in the blinded format, yet clearly went into trance to interact with St. James.

Medium 2002 was similarly difficult to categorize. She is also a psychic medium, yet she answered the questions in a blinded format and seemed to go into a trance to contact a blue universal consciousness that appeared to be a guide for humanity. Most of her session involved a low-level entity familiar to her, a teacher of children.

Medium 0001 was the "test" medium to see if the protocol would be successful before engaging the Fort Wayne and Charleston mediums. Her results are included for reasons explained in the Discussion section. She thoroughly answered all four questions, working only from the numbers without further prompts.

Blinded versus Nonblinded sessions

Five psychic mediums could not answer the questions in a blinded format, so as per the protocol, they were asked the questions directly.

The three full trance mediums answered the questions as numbers without further prompts. Follow-ups were done to obtain specific answers.

Nine mental mediums and two psychic mediums initially answered the questions in the blinded format. When the monitor was certain they were talking to an entity that could answer the questions posed in the blinded format, specific questions were asked.

Psychiatric Assessment of the Mediums

The study employed a Cartesian study approach, seeking to understand the psychological personality profiles of the mediums. Although psychometric measurement methods were used, the focus was on personality profiling rather than psychological or psychiatric diagnoses, as follows:

The average age was 44 years. Gender was 62.5% female. Over half did not have a partner. The average age at which they perceived they had abilities was 16. 87% felt their abilities increased with age. 81% had relatives with similar abilities. Commonly engaged senses were hearing (56.3%), touch (56.3%), and vision (50%). The study used the MCMI-IV personality disorder inventory and the Steinberg Disassociation inventory. The mediums had no evidence of psychopathology or personality disorders. The consulting forensic psychiatrist concluded that their dissociation during trance was benign and allowed them to access other realities.

The Entities

Allan Kardec emphasized that for wisdom acquisition, which is the goal of this project, one must be careful to only work with entities of the highest spiritual nature. (Kardec 2017 pp 85-101)

The 12 core mediums contacted only entities of the highest spiritual nature, with the oldest and most powerful spiritual pedigrees. Five of them contacted "The I Am." One medium contacted "the informational Universe," consistent with her understanding of the nature of God. She also mentioned "Prajivata."

One met the Holy Trinity and one St. James. Another met senior angels of the highest level with names such as "Atelier," "Andron," and "Baldrich." Several mediums met a host of unseen and unnamed sources who identified themselves as universal sources of wisdom. One said, "I am the all who is one."

Two mediums met the same entity named "Tabitha." Although having a prosaic name, Tabitha was described as a woman dressed in white from whom light emitted. Tabitha stated that she was located within a specific church from Allan Kardec's time in rural England but was also "everywhere." One medium said she was in contact with a buzzing electrical static noise outside her right ear. She then went into full trance, and the monitor asked the buzzing sound directly what its name was. It replied, "I am the I AM". When asked why it presented as a buzzing sound outside of the medium's head, the reply was, "(the medium) doesn't believe in me, so I stay close to her, outside but still close."

Other presentations included conscious bubbles who could speak, entities with large teeth who were scary, and an array of humanoid entities described as interdimensional beings. They also appeared to be of a high level as none of these manifestations were connected or associated with worldly material interests.

It was typical after a session for these mediums to state that they did not want to end the session and felt that they were in the presence of God, even if God presented simply as a roaring fire in a fireplace.

In contrast, the seven psychic mediums (two in Charleston and five in Fort Wayne) did not contact any higher-order entities. One exception: a medium who was nonblinded and otherwise spoke conversationally of his spirit guides suddenly and briefly went into a trance, stated he was "the I Am," and had a personal message for the monitor.

The psychic mediums contacted various personal guides, animal guides, spirit guides, and inner voices. All these entities had firm roots in this material world and spoke of worldly issues, including politics, culture, religious belief systems, and personal moral and ethical viewpoints. All these fit firmly within Kardec's descriptions of lower-order spirits.

No input was discarded. The psychic mediums had important and powerful fragments and pieces of a larger picture. However, they could not access or understand the higher-order expansive view of the spirit world that the core mediums presented.

The entities were engaged with the project and frequently had personal messages for the investigators. Several had specific messages encouraging the BICS team. Several entities made their appearances through trance mediums, such as the mother of one of the investigators and the great-aunt of another. Sometimes, the mediums amusingly chided them to leave and not "hijack" the session.

Summary of Entities Contacted

Twelve core trance mediums, 8 in Fort Wayne and 4 in Charleston, contacted entities of the highest spiritual order. They received a broad overview of the answers to the questions, placed within the greater context of how the spirit world guides and inspires humanity for spiritual progress. They commented on the more significant concepts, such as how spiritual inspirations for technology and science lead to spiritual progression. They clarified their relationship to the Earth humans inhabit, the nature of reality, and the entangled and intermingled relationship between the spirit world, its interdimensional partners, and humanity. They discussed precisely how mediums communicate with entities in both metaphorical and precise mathematic terms and went out of their way to affirm the project's working scientific model. This led, for example, to a high school graduate in Fort Wayne who has no advanced mathematic training discussing $1/f$ frequencies with the monitor.

The seven psychic mediums contacted entities of a low spiritual nature, including those who might be considered earthbound spirits. Not surprisingly, many of these appeared as "ghosts" to those psychic mediums who were also paranormal investigators.

Table One: Information about Mediums

Locale	Medium	Medium Type	Entities Contacted	Prior Contact	Blinded
FW	0101	Psychic	Inner Voice	Yes	No
FW	0102	Mental	I Am the I Am	No	Yes
FW	0103	Psychic	Personal Guides, Penelope	Yes	No
FW	0106	Trance	The Trinity	No	Yes
FW	0108	Psychic	Inner Voices	Yes	No
FW	0109	Psychic	Damon, unnamed lower level entities	No	Yes
FW	0110	Trance	Angels, including Baldwick, Andron	No	Yes
FW	0112	Mental	God-like voice	No	Yes
FW	0113	Mental	Tabitha (an angel)	Yes	Yes
FW	0114	Mental	I Am the I Am, Intelligent bubbles	No	Yes

FW	0115	Mental	The All That is One	No	Yes
FW	0116	Mental	The Gatekeeper	No	Yes
CH	0117	Mental	I Am the I AM	No	Yes
CH	2002	Psychic	Blue Conscious Guide, Also a teacher of children	No	Yes
CH	2003	Psychic	St James	No	No
CH	2004	Mental/ Trance	They Who Are One And "God"	No	Yes
CH	2005	Mental	Tabitha (an angel)	No	Yes
CH	2006	Psychic	Inner Voices	Yes	No
CH	2007	Trance	The entity did not give a name but appeared to be "God" or a universal voice of authority	Yes	Yes

"Trance" indicates a medium that went into full trance and with the entity speaking directly to the monitor.

"Mental" indicates a bilocated trance medium that spoke both to the entity and to the monitor, acting as an intermediate between the two.

"Psychic" means a medium that does not directly contact entities but rather is influenced and receives information through an "inner voice" or directly from a low-level entity such as a spirit guide. As indicated, sometimes, psychics go into a full trance while answering the questions.

How Were the Medium Sessions Assessed?

All sessions were videotaped with transcriptions initially created by Rev.com. One set of monitors interviewed the Fort Wayne mediums; a different set interviewed the Charleston mediums. An independent outside attorney observed many of the sessions to ensure that leading questions were not used and to certify the integrity of the sessions. The forensic psychiatrist also observed many of the sessions and acted as a monitor at times.

The project's priority was presenting the 4 BICS questions to the mediums. One way to conceptualize this project is that it is an update of Allan Kardec's Book of the Spirits (Kardec 2017). The project essentially asks the Other Side for a progress report on what has happened since then.

Yet how can it be verified that the mediums have contacted a discarnate entity instead of sharing creations of their own consciousness and mind/brain?

Kardec stated that the nature of the information itself is proof of its providence. He states that humans all have a source of wisdom within themselves that is connected to the greater informational universe, a source that is often referred to as one's "inner voice" or "teacher within." That "teacher" can evaluate the information obtained from mediums and discern if it is genuine wisdom acquired from The Other Side for the benefit of humanity. Yet this distinction between information from a discarnate entity and the medium's biases and spiritual understandings can be challenging to differentiate precisely.

The team is not suggesting that the selected mediums would intentionally con anyone or be disingenuous in their presentations. Instead, all mediums constantly struggle to tell the difference between what is from their own mind/brain and what information is contained in the greater Universe they are accessing. (Kardec 1876 pp 98-102) (Kardec 2017 pp 34-42)

That is why the study's mediums enjoy the training exercises of Spiritual Sight, as immediate feedback is given after a session. The medium can learn to distinguish the psychic "feel" of information from a universal source and what is invented by their mind/brain.

Therefore, the project's first approach was to apply Kardec's criteria. The tests he proposed for the information included: Does it seem to be of a higher spiritual nature? Are the language and concepts utilized in harmony with someone of the highest spiritual level? Does it match what one's inner teacher/intuition thinks is true?"

Yet, as Kardec acknowledged, this has limitations in that humans have biases, cultural and spiritual belief systems, and prejudices, all of which can cloud one's inner assessment. Therefore, as discussed below, Kardec's criteria were modified for this project.

The precise nature of the answers and how the medium obtained those answers were carefully examined.

The scientists' working metaphor is the digital stacking of photographic plates used in astronomy and astrophysics to image faint objects optimally in the distant skies. Astronomers used to stack glass plates and now stack digital images, some with little information on them or others crowded with images from the Universe, and then look at the entire stack as one portrait of the distant skies. Astrophysicists use this technique to minimize signal-to-noise interference. (Knox R)

The same problem is present in the signal-to-noise problem in interpreting information from the mediums. It is unknown what the most critical information is and what should be discarded as "noise." No data from the mediums was discarded as it was found that all fit into a coherent, powerful message for humanity. The core trance mediums were the most accurate "telescopes" with the deepest penetration into the mysterious universe. The psychic mediums, who demonstrated competence in Spiritual Sight, presented bits and pieces and often powerful fragments that complemented the core mediums' work.

For example, all the mediums referenced an age-old struggle between two complementary yet antagonistic forces in the spiritual world. This is often conceptualized as "light and dark" or "good and evil." In human terms, the metaphors used to describe this endlessly shifting and evolving dynamic through the millennia are often "angels and devils," "sinners and saints," and so forth. Allan Kardec stated that each medium has its own vocabulary and metaphors depending on their life histories and cultural/religious background; this is one reason they often superficially appear to be giving different answers. The team saw this in the responses to the BICS question 1, discussed below, where all the mediums had essentially the same answer. Yet, some said "yes" and some said "no" depending on their conceptualizations of the language of the question.

The mediums indicated that humanity is at a dark place in its spiritual evolution, suggesting that humanity has failed to progress and might even be at risk of self-extinction. The core mediums presented this but put it in the context of a greater struggle throughout human history and emphasized that the time since Allan Kardec is a blink of an eye in the spirit world. "We tend to take the thousand-year view" is one entity's statement. This is appropriate as it is often forgotten that humans have existed in their current form for at least several hundred thousand years. (Hardwerk B)

Several psychic mediums only saw the current darkness and struggle. One focused entirely on this struggle in his answers. Instead of the metaphors of angels and ghosts as has often been used in prior ages, the metaphor of interdimensional beings and even "angels" of the departed spirits of those interdimensional beings was used, the conflict framed as an immediate and epic battle going on unseen by humanity. His contribution was vitally important as he focused solely on the current struggle around us, whereas the core mediums often spoke of the battle without specifics. The psychic mediums were all presented with complementary fragments by their entities that could only be understood using the "stacked plate approach" used in deep space astronomy to image the heavens above correctly.

THE MEDIUMS

1. 13 FROM FORT WAYNE, 6 FROM CHARLESTION
2. 12 TRANCE MEDIUMS
3. 7 PSYCHIC MEDIUMS
4. FROM ALL WALKS OF LIFE AND BELIEF SYSTEMS
5. THE 12 TRANCE MEDIUMS ANSWERED THE QUESTIONS AS NUMBERS.
6. THE 7 PSYCHIC MEDIUMS ANSWERED THE QUESTIONS AS WRITTEN.
7. ALL DEMONSTRATED PROFICIENCY IN SPIRITUAL SITE AND COULD MOVE ELECTRONS WITH THEIR MINDS

Did the Mediums Contact Discarnate Entities?

The Spirits validated their communications, highlighting how important they considered their message.

The BICS questions are somewhat skeptical and demanding in nature. One medium, who dropped out early on, objected to the problematic wording and tone of the questions, stating that TOS must be approached using the highest spiritual language. Yet again and again, the entities knew precisely what was being asked, stated that they were part of the framing of the questions, directly inspired the BICS Challenge Grant, and would provide as much internal validation of the answers as possible. For example, one medium, also an agent for the United States Federal Bureau of Investigation, was given the number for one of the BICS questions. She went into a trance and stated that a woman was approaching her. "She is holding something; it's stone, curved on the top, square at the bottom. There are ten markings on it, markings I can't read". She was shown the 10 Commandments carved in stone, indisputable proof that she contacted an entity as the question clearly asked for such an answer.

The number she was given corresponds to the second BICS question, which asks the spirit world to document with specifics how it has helped humanity. BICS charged the ISSC's experimental design with holding the spirit world's feet to the fire and getting specifics from them that would stand up in a Court of Law. The Spirit World took the challenge and openly rebuked the skeptical tone of Question 2 by presenting the Ten Commandments as their first piece of evidence. The Ten Commandments are arguably one of the most powerful instructions from the Spirit World for man's progress.

This illustrates how the questions presented as numbers help determine which part of the answer comes from the spirit world and which is from the medium's mind/brain. The numbers contain no hint as to the nature of the question, so they decrease mental noise that could be created from these questions, which basically ask whose fault it is for the current climate of wars, violence, and hatred seen worldwide.

The neuroscience of mediumship makes it clear why even experienced and well-trained mediums have difficulty sorting out this internal mental noise problem. The project's working model of consciousness is that information that comes to the brain through non-ordinary means, such as Spiritual Sight or mediumship, hacks the existing perceptual system and plugs the non-ordinary information into the current information processing system. Neuroscientist David Eagleman describes a similar approach in his work with blind individuals. He takes the same information contained in visual imagery. He translates it into tactile information by having the subjects wear abdominal vests, which code braille-like signals into input to the mind/brain's optical system. Eventually, these research subjects will start to "see" even though the information is given to them through their skin. This example demonstrates that the brain is driven to process information and create one's inner mental reality, even if that information comes through non-ordinary means. (Eagleman D pp 55-90))

Once the neuroscience of mediumship is understood, it becomes clear why conversations with discarnate entities are hard to distinguish from the medium's inner dialogue. Since the information is plugged into and processed by the existing perceptual system, the experience often seems just as real as one's ordinary perceptions of local reality. However, these experiences are not part of one's internal mental model of reality. It is Neuroscience 101 that the mind/brain does not directly perceive the world but instead creates a cognitive model of reality from sensory input from non-local reality, which is processed as electrochemical signals transmitted to the mind/brain. (Eagleman D & Barden G)

It is the mind/brain's mental model of reality that seems "real." Over the years, this mental model has been created by interacting with other humans and their personal local reality. For example, children are taught which wavelengths of light correspond to "red," a very labor-intensive task, as any parent knows. Colors, of course, do not exist in nature. (Eagleman D p 84) So, to visualize something as "red," one must create a visual image corresponding to the image others have when they state something is "red." This is what is meant by the mind/brain's mental model.

There is, however, no community-accepted inner mental model that corresponds to spiritual information that comes from non-local reality through non-ordinary means. So, it seems odd, strange, or unreal. As the child who had a near-death experience said of his experiences in non-local reality, "It was real, Dr. Morse, it was realer than real." By this, he meant that although it had the exact perceptual "feel" as any other perception, it did not match with anything in his interior mental model, so it seemed strange or unreal.

Spiritual Sight is a training tool to help mediums understand this subtle but clear-cut difference in thoughts from non-local reality and those from the medium's mind/brain's local reality. However, it takes years to perceive the difference quickly and easily, often only achieved by Masters of Spiritual Sight. As a result, especially for highly emotionally charged spiritual questions directed to The Other Side, it is extremely difficult for either the monitor or the medium to determine which information came from a discarnate entity and which from the inevitable effort of the medium's mind/brain also to answer the question. This is the rationale behind presenting the questions as numbers.

TOS Presented Validation Within the Information Presented

The BICS questions have a skeptical tone. As a result, the Other Side often embedded validation within the answers. They tried to provide the specifics necessary to answer the four questions to a level that could be presented in a (hypothetical) court of law.

For example, one medium in Fort Wayne contacted an entity named Tabitha. She lived in a church in England in Allan Kardec's time, but she also "is everywhere." She was the highest-order entity. The medium came in contact with her after being given the number for the first question. She described being in the small rural English village, meeting a sizeable, officious man who was too busy to talk to her, and pointing her to Tabitha as someone who could answer her questions. Tabitha was a tall woman dressed in white and radiant. The medium had the sense of being with God when she spoke with her.

Tabitha told her, "Failure leads to progress" as the answer to the first question. The medium did not know the question yet gave an answer referencing Kardec's time and the nature of progress and failure.

A medium in Charleston was given the same number for the question, interacted with the same entity, Tabitha, and was given the same answer. In other words, she was contacted by the same entity that had interacted with the Fort Wayne medium. The medium was taken to the same place as the Fort Wayne medium, a rural village in England during the time of Allan Kardec. She met the same entities described by the Fort Wayne mediums, entered a church, and was introduced to a woman dressed in white who emanated a white light. She said her name was Tabitha. She answered the questions as she had previously answered when they were presented through the Fort Wayne medium.

When presented with such astonishing validation of the integrity of the process, it is natural to wonder if the mediums somehow colluded and faked this result. The history of scientific investigation of mediumship has shown that mediums can dupe well-intentioned scientists (Thompkins M). That is why the protocol included a forensic psychiatrist and an outside attorney involved in the sessions' protocol and monitoring. Both mediums have been thoroughly investigated, and there is no evidence or conceivable way they could have colluded.

When the spirit world was presented with Question 3, which essentially asks the spirit world, "What have they done for us lately?" there followed an avalanche of evidence presented through the mediums.

For example, upon being given the number for question 3, one medium drew a picture of the benzene ring. She had no idea of the molecular structure of benzene or its significance. She was a high school graduate living in middle America. She also described seeing red threads. Again, she had no idea why that was important and even expressed surprise at seeing the threads.

The German chemist Kukele was shown the structure of the benzene ring in a vision while in a dreamy half-asleep state in 1886. (Rocke A. Chapter 10) Benzene became an important industrial chemical used to develop aniline dyes for fabric. The first color produced was bright scarlet. The invention of aniline dyes led directly to Germany's industrial might at the turn of the 19th century and is arguably an essential part of Germany's wars of expansion in the early 20th century. (Travis T) As will be seen, the spirit world has been clear that it is responsible for such conflicts as they are moral and spiritual growth opportunities for humankind. For example, World War 1 led to the League of Nations, an early precursor to The United Nations.

When presented with the same number, a different medium was shown: a glass tube with mercury in it. The mercury was in the tube, and there were markings on the side. The medium was unaware that the mercury thermometer was invented by David Fahrenheit as "an answer to prayer." The thermometer was an essential part of the scientific revolution of the 18th century; however, that occurred in 1714 (Fahrenheit D 1724), which is not the time period of the question.

So, the medium may have been referring to the invention of the first practical medical thermometer, which radically transformed the practice of medicine, impacting the diagnosis and treatment of everything from infectious diseases to the management of surgical patients. This was invented by Sir Thomas Clifford Allbutt in 1867, which is within the time period of the question. Sir Allbutt was described as a "spiritual aristocrat." He believed that his many medical and scientific achievements resulted in his finding the mysteries of God's law in the human body and the natural world. (Chance B)

Two of the mediums contacted the spirit of Allan Kardec and asked him the BICS questions. Again, they worked entirely from a number yet were contacted by a spirit who precisely fit the description of Allan Kardec.

For example, one of the mediums immediately stated that the number was associated with a dead man and accurately described Allan Kardec.

The other mediums drew a steamer trunk from the 1800s and called it The Trunk of Knowledge. She said the entity she contacted stated that for humankind's spiritual progress to continue, the Trunk of Knowledge must be opened. At that point, she had worked solely from the number corresponding to the question.

Some Spiritists call Allan Kardec's five books the Trunk of Knowledge. The term "trunk of knowledge" is not found in English translations of his work. The term "trunk" is based on the French word "trunc," often used as a metaphor for the Tree of Knowledge in French.

One final example came from a medium who, in answering Question 1, presented the Spirit World's influence on both the planet and humanity's spiritual progress. She was shown a vision of the Earth, surrounded by two hands holding it between them. They were moving rhythmically close and then away from the Earth. The monitor recognized the movement of the medium's hands as she demonstrated how the hands moved while holding the planet, the characteristic rhythm associated with the quantum waves that connect us, and the unmistakable signature of the 1/f frequency. Theoretical physicists and cognitive neuroscientists have described this 1/f frequency as the physical signature of consciousness. (Pitkaanen M 2001)(Anderson C 2000)

The BICS investigators stressed that they wanted specific answers to the questions that could be independently verified as coming from The Other Side. The ISSC protocol of presenting the questions as numbers to the mediums is one method of blinding the mediums to the nature of the investigation and ensuring the integrity of the process.

IV Results

A.- BICS Question One: Answers

The answers given by the mediums to the first question:

"Since 1857, has the Other Side failed and Mankind failed to achieve good progress in securing human spirituality? If so, are bad spirits and bad humans winning?"

A1.- Yes and No Answers

Mediums who answered yes: 10

(0106, 0108, 0109, 0113, 0112, 0116, 0117, 2002, 2005, 2006)

Mediums who answered no: 6

(0102, 0115, 0110, 0114, 2003, 2004)

Mediums with undetermined answers: 3

(0101, 0103, 2007)

Core trance mediums: 8 answered "yes," 3 answered "no," and 1 was undetermined.

Psychic mediums: 2 answered "yes," 3 answered "no," and 2 undetermined.

Consensus Viewpoint

The consensus, especially among the core trance mediums, is that humanity has failed to make good progress in securing human spirituality since 1857. All agree that humans are to blame yet acknowledge that humanity's failure is the spirit world's failure, in the sense that when a child fails, the parent has also failed.

The best overview of the consensus answer was Medium 0115, who, after receiving the question's number, responded: "The nature of the world is so you can choose. It is designed so that human beings can progress in their souls and their spirit. And that requires challenge, temptation, bad things happening, what you call bad. So, it's not a matter of winning or losing. It is a matter of it's all there together, and it's essential for the human journey."

A2.- Progress Through Failure

Although the responses to the first question seem divided at first glance, with a predominance of affirmative answers, a deeper analysis reveals a more complex picture. Rather than one side prevailing over the other, as presented below, the mediums' insights collectively suggest that various experiences, including perceived setbacks, contribute to humanity's spiritual progress.

When Medium 2005 was presented with the First Question's corresponding number, the contacted entity immediately said, "Progress through failure."

When given the number for the same question, one of the entities contacted by Medium 0108 immediately said, "Hatred blocks progress."

After receiving the corresponding number, Medium 0001's entity stated, "The problem is not that something is winning or losing, but that we think in terms of winning and losing. We cannot make progress when we divide into winning and losing. We must return to oneness (…) Nature is one, and we cannot divide one (…) We must return to oneness, to virtue, to stop forcing ourselves on the world but to live with it as one."

Medium 2002 also acknowledged that "We are at a time of a great awakening (…) Although mankind has not progressed as it could, they still have progressed, and failure is part of that process."

As Medium 2002 explained. "This reality is a school," and responded affirmatively, "Yes, however, we are at a time of a great awakening... People's awareness is going to be blossoming left and right. It's going to come very quickly to them and so many that have never experienced any type of awareness"

A3.- Humans Are Failing

Seemingly questioning the relevance of the concept of "winning" in the spiritual realm, Medium 0115 responded to the first question with another question: "What is winning?"

Medium 0113's entity stated that "bad people and bad spirits are (currently) winning," although "not totally," and that "there is volatility, different positions, bad spirits in the political realm...". "Bad spirits win by deceit," but the implication is that humans do not have to believe their lies.

Regarding who is to blame, Medium 0117 bluntly explained that behind this failure are "humans, not spirits, bad humans."

When asked if the bad humans were winning, Medium 0114 had a vision of a "narrow balance beam," with "danger on either side, crocodiles on one, piranhas on the other. Fear is holding humans back. I can't progress on the balance beam, I am afraid, I'm getting a sense of losing perspective. Maybe even losing morality."

Medium 0117's entity said that behind this failure, there are "humans, not spirits, bad humans."

As one of the entities contacted by Medium 2006 explained, "Humans are responsible for their slowed development in the past 150 years. Bad spirits are not working against humanity; they are doing it with their own egos."

Medium 0115 hints at the situation's complexity with these words: "But now the earth is on the precipice of teetering into dark times because the world is filled with those whose goals are not love, are not caring, are not humanity. They are selfish. They need to move on in their journeys for them to grow. Unfortunately, some of those humans are in powerful positions. However, all is not lost. There is a strong basis of love in your world. There is a strong sense of compassion or human dignity."

Medium 0110 sustained, "Humans themselves are holding themselves back by not having empathy for others, by not choosing love, by not learning and communicating with each other, especially people we don't understand or like."

A4: Humans Have Not Failed

Medium 2003's entity stated, "No one has failed, but things should have turned out differently (…) Bad humans and bad spirits are not winning (…) Progress is made (…) Stop judging yourself thinking you should be further ahead or further behind. Failure is only fear; stop your fear with love." When asked how things could have turned out differently, the entity only stated: "peace."

Medium 2004's said, "You have not failed. There is no such thing. More and more of you are waking up, and we're so excited. Keep spreading the word and the love. Has TOS failed in helping humans achieve spirituality? No, we have not failed. We're here giving you guidance every day, every minute. Unfortunately, some of you are caught up in the day-to-day physical, and you forget to stop and connect to love, which is us. We are here. We have not failed. No one has failed. Keep going."

Medium 0115's entity professed: "It is not a matter of winning or losing," while Medium 0116's mentioned that the terms "good and bad should not be used" since "the light needs shadow.

Medium 0115's entity further addressed the issue of "bad humans": "The answer is there is good and bad in everyone. Some people here in your world choose the difficult path that you call bad. But often, it's to help others learn and grow. Because even in bad actions there is a spark in everyone that connects to the whole. We have not failed. You have not failed. No one is winning; there is nothing to win."

The entity further addressed the issue of progress: "Progress is something that's measured in many different ways. The inhabitants of earth are the humans who are trying to find their way. They have a challenge, challenges before them. Progress to us is over time that is eternal. We do see there has been progress, and there will continue to be progress."

A5.- Human Progress is Non-Linear

Those who responded negatively seem to agree that significant progress has been made despite all the possible obstacles and drawbacks.

Most responses suggested a dynamic and non-linear understanding of spiritual development transcending the traditional binaries of success and failure or good and evil. Instead, they indicate that everything is part of a continuous growth, learning, and adaptation process. This highlights the importance of facing challenges and making choices, implying that what is perceived as 'bad' or negative can be crucial for spiritual progress.

This suggests that what may be perceived as 'bad' or negative experiences are crucial for spiritual growth and that challenges, difficulties, and even adversities are not merely obstacles but essential elements in the journey of spiritual growth. These challenges are seen not as hindrances but as catalysts for growth and opportunities for learning, and they are necessary for the evolution of the human spirit.

As Medium 0001 expressed, there seems to reign a sense of unity and shared purpose, "Nature is one, and we cannot divide one (…) We must return to oneness, to virtue, to stop forcing ourselves on the world but to live with it as one."

A6.- Human Progress is Cyclical

Many responses suggested that human progress is a cyclical process, marked by periods of awakening, introspection, and even setbacks considered integral to humanity's overall development.

Medium 0114's entity noted, "Neither side is winning, the pattern constantly shifts (...) It's all working out, everything is working out as it should. It's a balance, and it's two sides of a coin."

Medium 0106's expressed: "The answer is that we are on a roller coaster, or a conveyor belt, going up and down, up and down, but no one is losing; eventually, everyone is winning (...) There was a time of great spiritual awakening; then, humanity became closed off to Spirit, and now, it is waking up again. Right now is the worst it has ever been; that is correct."

These answers underscore the ongoing struggle and the fluid nature of spiritual challenges, indicating they are part of the spiritual journey.

A7.-Allan Kardec's Views on the Matter

In "The Spirit's Book," Allan Kardec held the same nuanced view of human spiritual development as the entities who responded to Question 1. Kardec is responding to the subtext of question 1, which asks why there are so many wars and calamities in the present time, implying that the horrific events indicate a lack of progress.

"Calamities are trials that furnish humans with an opportunity to exert their intelligence and to demonstrate their patience and resignation before the will of God. At the same time, calamities enable them to develop the sentiments of self-denial, self-detachment, and love for their neighbor – if they are not dominated by selfishness" (Kardec, 2006, p. 413-414)

"If during our time on earth we often choose the most difficult trials with a view to evolving further, why would a spirit who sees even farther down the road and for whom earthly life is only a fleeting incident not choose a painful and laborious existence if it will lead it toward eternal happiness?" (Kardec, 2006, p. 220)

"After each existence, they see the steps they have already taken and understand what they lack in purity to reach the goal. That is the reason why they willingly submit to all the vicissitudes of corporeal life, even requesting the ones that will help them arrive more quickly" (Kardec, 2006, p. 219)

Kardec's words highlight that spiritual growth is inherently linked with facing and overcoming challenges and adversities. This coincides with most mediums' entities, who seemed to conclude that spiritual growth is not a straightforward path but a rich tapestry of experiences, choices, and transitions, all contributing to the evolution of the human spirit.

The Risk of Self-Inflicted Extinction (Supplemental Question 2)

Supplemental question 2 is a natural follow-up to Question 1. It is: **"Without some shift in planet-wide spirituality to match technological growth, humans on this planet are at risk of self-inflicted extinction. If you agree with this statement, please give specific remedies. If you disagree, please give us specific reasons."**

Although not a direct answer to question one, the ISSC team would be remiss in not including the entitys' answer to this question. Regardless of whether they answered "yes" or "no" to whether humanity is progressing spiritually, all indicated that humans are at risk of self-extinction. These answers were embedded in their answers to Question 1, so it is appropriate that they be presented here.

Medium 0001 said she had a vision and said, "Tobacco? The smell of tobacco and fields of tobacco. It all can go in smoke. We force tobacco into our lungs; we can't force nature to be what it does not want to be."

Medium 0112 said she felt strange, "I feel like I just watched a car wreck... That feeling like, I don't know how to describe that. It's not that I saw; I mean, at one point, I got a glimpse of war, and I don't know if it was just talking about the past or if it's something that's going to end up happening, but I just have this feeling of I just witnessed a wreck, and I don't know if the people are okay."

Medium 0113, after being given the numbers corresponding to question 1, stated that a woman approached her, saying: "I can answer the question. The answer is yes.

(Medium) A woman is watching.

(Monitor) What is her name? (Medium) Tabitha.

(Medium): She is watching people and watching people over (other) people. She is sad. She is missing something. Oh its her head. Metaphorically. She is missing some part of herself. She is in Victorian dress, 1850s. Name is Tamara, or Tabitha. She is missing her family, those close to her makes her happy.

She will only say the answer to the question is yes; both parts are yes.

(The Medium): I have a sudden feeling of being carefree, wild, raw, wind is blowing my hair. And we (humanity) are going off a cliff and then going to die. This is a warning (says Tabitha/Tamara) Being wild and free and where it gets you. Freedom is needed, not feeling free.

Remedies: Supplemental Question 2

Again, these remedies were typically included in the answers to Question 1. Appendix 1 presents a full report of all the supplemental and additional questions.

In brief, the entities state that humanity's lack of faith and failure to integrate spiritual understandings into everyday lives has caused the problems. This is particularly seen in technology, as once scientists sought God's plan in the natural world. Today's science has far outstripped human morality and ethics and is not guided by TOS to advance spiritual progress. The remedies require a return to faith, to reject hate and fear, and to embrace empathy and love. As one entity stated: "They (humans) must look through the eyes of the other."

B.- BICS Question Two: Answers

The following presents the answers given by the mediums to the second question:

"Explain to people on Earth why the Other Side has not failed in fostering spiritual evolution."

The following answers to the second question reveal what the TOS had to say on this matter:

B1.- No One has Failed

Several mediums highlighted that spiritual evolution is not about "failing" or "succeeding." Instead, they view it as a continuous and unified universal process that humanity cannot understand.

As Medium 0001 explained after being given the number for the second question: "We have not failed, humankind has not failed. (You) don't understand what progress is or how it occurs. We (humanity) are the blob, and the spirit world is the higher order. It can only try to shape us, but parts of the blob cannot fit or understand the higher configuration."

Medium 2004's entity alleged, "We have not failed, neither have you. You as people give too much notice to your fear and not enough to love and the joy and the fun and the friendship, the connection you have with others."

Accordingly, Medium 0115 expressed, "Humanity has not failed in spiritual evolution, and we have not failed you."

Medium 2002's entity stated, "There is no failure. Consciousness has to evolve as it's ready to. You cannot judge how that happens. Humans are so locked into everything being right or wrong, and it's only now that you're finally starting to see the massive lifetimes of duality that you are starting to break free from you."

Medium 0115's entity expressed, "Humanity has not failed in spiritual evolution, and we have not failed you. The best example of progress is the development of civilization... When humankind makes progress, the spirit world makes progress. They are one and the same, indicating no failure on either side."

Some participants, including Medium 0116, also considered this unity between humans and the other side, who stated, "Help is always there, but humans don't ask for it... The spirit world and the human world evolve together and are, in fact, one."

Medium 0113 specified why The Other Side has not failed as follows, "They have not failed because they continuously try to reach us (humans). And some of us they do and they know and they gravitate towards us because they feel like we are the messengers and they keep trying to help people keep bad spirits away. I feel like a lot of people don't have the other side on their side, and that's because of the disconnect."

B2.- Mankind has Failed to Listen to TOS

Despite the previous views, and although there has been no complete failure, The entity contacted by Medium 0101 said, "It is the physical side of Earth that is failing (...) We (humans) don't understand what is progress, how it occurs, we are the blob, the spirit world is the higher order, it can only try to shape us, but parts of the blob cannot fit or understand the higher configuration (...) The reason that humanity has not progressed is a failure of (human) leadership and religion (the spiritual side)."

Medium 0108's entity pointed out that "Mankind has failed to make progress" because "The spirit world has tried to help, but people generally do not want to listen," blaming it on "a loss of faith, a lack of belief in the spirit world."

Medium 0106 emphasized this, stating that upon being given the number for the question, she was approached by a woman who showed her a tablet of stone with ten lines of writing on it that she couldn't read. The implication is that we have ignored the guidance of the Ten Commandments.

Medium 0112's explained, "It's not TOS's fault. You can lead a horse to water. They give us the tools. We've shunned information. We've turned our noses up at information out of fear and ego and what we deem as important. Humans have taken the wrong road code. I don't want to say the rock road. We've gone off course…"

As Medium 2007 stated, "It is not the spirit side that has failed. It's the choices of those in the physical.

Similarly, Medium 0108 points out that the leading cause of this failure is humans "don't want to listen" to the Other Side: "Mankind has failed to make progress. The spirit world has tried to help, but people generally do not want to listen. The main problem is a loss of faith, a lack of belief in the spirit world."

In summary, according to most entities, the reasons for this apparent failure are diverse, ranging from fear and not fully engaging with the opportunities for spiritual growth to a lack of faith, ignorance of spiritual tools, and distraction by material pursuits.

Achieving spiritual evolution mostly depends on humanity, as explained by Medium 0110: "Humanity had to move around the Earth, discover new ideas, work together for survival, find their place as one people, one humanity. Be humble, realize that nature is bigger than humankind, and change their relationship with the Earth to be humbler and more spiritual."

B3.- How the Other Side Has Helped

As confirmed by most mediums, the Other Side, or Spiritual Realm, has helped, guided, inspired, or influenced humanity through different forms of intervention. This guidance is often seen as a subtle influence rather than a direct intervention, suggesting spiritual mentorship or guardianship.

Medium 0117's entity flatly stated: "Everything. Everything humans have accomplished is because of the spirit world." Medium 0115's entity agreed, saying, "Anything done that is good is because of spirit."

Medium 2005 stated, "They allow humankind's spirituality to grow. They 'nudge' humans."

Medium 2003's entity, presented with the number corresponding to the question, gave several specific examples of how the spirit world has helped humans progress spiritually. 1) The Earth itself was given to humanity by the spirit world. 2) Reincarnation. Death and rebirth are essential for spiritual progress. 3) Religion. Religion was supposed to help people find wisdom within, but they transformed it into something different. "Humans got in the way and changed the answers. They failed the test of religion (as it was originally presented to us). 4) Science. Science is to guide us. The technology of the Iron Age led to religion. (this was shown to the medium as a vision of past events)

Medium 2006 briefly answered the same question: "Jesus was a prophet, brought to earth to advance mankind."

Medium 0114 had a vision of "dropping lanterns" and said the Spirit World has lit the path by dropping these, metaphorically speaking: "They are dropping lanterns, and some turn into fires…" The Monitor asked, "Into fires?" "Yes," responded the medium. "I get the sense that that's when the… it's almost like the actual communication happens when there's a fire. There's an actual breakthrough. The lantern has caught the fuel source (…) It's sort of the idea of a flash of insight or brilliance or improvement when there's a great leap forward in personal knowledge or science or in other places (…) It's a metaphor (…) I get the sense that it's the actual communication happening. I see. It's the combustion of both elements coming together. I don't know how to interpret that." The Monitor then asked, "Can you give a specific example?" and the medium replied, "I saw a sidewalk," as well as "thousands of songs."

During her trance, Medium 0106 had a vision of a tall cylinder. The Monitor asked her to describe it, and she said it was a glass cylinder with numbers on one of its sides: "There was mercury," she explained. The Monitor asked where the mercury was, and the reply was, "It was on the inside." The same medium also had a vision containing symbolic imagery involving stone tablets.

It must be noted that Gabriel Fahrenheit expressed the following in his 1724 '*Experimenta circa gradum caloris*,' "When a (mercury) thermometer … was made (perhaps imperfect in many ways*) the result answered to my prayer*; and with great pleasure of mind, I observed the truth (that water boils at a fixed degree of heat)." (Fahrenheit D) The thermometer's invention led directly to innumerable advances in all areas of science, including medicine, chemistry, and physics.

When Medium 0110 was asked when the Other Side has helped humankind, he stated that this has happened "many, many times." One example she gave was the Ice Age: "It changed how humans progressed towards the ultimate goal of the universe."

Medium 0103 said, regarding how they have helped us, "The spirit world does not foster spiritual evolution but guides humanity individually. People think that they come up with random ideas, but these are inspired by spirit."

Medium 0113's entity illustrates this with the spirit world's response to school shootings: "Tabitha says that they're watching and they tried to push the gunmen, but the only thing that they can reach is the people inside of schools or buildings or churches to react in a certain way."

Medium 0115's entity emphasized the role of human choices in advancing their spiritual progress. "We go back to what we said in the beginning, which is that there is good and bad in every human being. It is how that human chooses to connect with spirit or not connect with one that will help determine whether they go forth in light or in darkness. And many are afraid. They don't know. They can't allow themselves to open themselves to spirit. What you call bad is not spirit, it's lack of spirit. The dark side is the lack of spirit.

B4.- Connection With the Other Side

Most mediums mention a close relationship between humanity and The Other Side.

Medium 0115's entity said, "When Mankind makes progress, the spirit world makes progress. They are the same, indicating no failure on either side (…). The spiritual world is not separate from Mankind. We are all connected. We are all a part of the whole. And while we are not humans, we care about humans because you're a part of us, but not in the way that humans necessarily sense because time is very different. Time is a human construct. It's not of this place."

The same entity added that this connection or unity is more profound in some people: "They understand they are in touch, and those are the people who begin to make huge changes for humanity. There are people like Gandhi; there are people like Nelson Mandela, people like Martin Luther King Jr. whose spirits are so connected and so strong that they pour through them from us."As Medium 0116 and others mentioned, "The spirit world and the human world evolve together, and are in fact one," therefore in reality there is no need for one to 'help' the other, for "they are all part of one whole."

Medium 0108 addressed the deeply personal relationship between the spirit world and humanity. Much of the spiritual progress occurs on a one-on-one level: "They can help protect you if you, like you've been in a car accident, but you and your car flipped, but you didn't suffer any scratch or burns or anything. They can protect you that way. It can, if you are starting to go down the wrong path in your life, they can make something happen that makes you open up your eyes and go, wait, what the hell was I just doing? Why am I trying to do that? I should be doing this."

Medium 2002's entity articulated the difficult concept that there is no separation between the spirit world and humanity, only different manifestations of energy:" It's a very human thing to think that once we're separate of our bodies, that what we consider spirit is still separate from the universal energies. It's all a blending. The energy is all you're ever present; it's all there all the time. We have created that duality, that separation to experience earth as earth is experienced, and just because what once was a spirit in any particular reality, even a light being that does not need to have a physical body but shows up as a presence of energy. That's how source is electing to portray that aspect of itself. What you consider a spirit, a soul is all source breaking off in whatever way it chooses to express itself. So you've broken off to be human in a human body, very dense. There are aspects of source that break off to embody an energy form that does not need a dense physical body. And that energy simply has consolidated to experience itself in this energetic form. So if it's already energy like you perceive your spirit or soul to be, and it already doesn't have a body in its reality."

B5.- What Allan Kardec Said

"We have already spoken to you of those worlds where the newborn soul is placed, when, still ignorant of good and evil, it can progress toward God, lord of itself, in possession of its free will. You have already been informed regarding the ample faculties given to the soul so that it may practice the good." (Kardec, 1987, p. 76).

C.- BICS Question Three: Answers

The following analysis considers the answers given by the mediums to the third question:

"What difference has the Other Side made in the past 166 years in influencing humans to accelerate their spiritual progress."

The core mediums indicated that the Other Side has actively influenced spiritual progress through inspiration, guidance, technological advancements, and direct spiritual experiences. Most highlight a symbiotic relationship between the spiritual and human realms that boosts spiritual progress in three primary areas:

It is important to note that most of the entities presented the answers to questions 2 and 3 as if they were the same question, although question 3 specifies the time period since 1867. As one entity stated: "We tend to take the long view, looking at a span of a thousand years."

C1.- Influence on Science and Technology

Many mediums mentioned that the Other Side has inspired critical technological and scientific breakthroughs. Examples include the inventions of Nikola Tesla and Thomas Edison, as well as discoveries like the benzene ring and blood types.

Medium 2003 was shown an array of scientific advances, "they all just flashed by, but seemingly all the inventions since 1857, the radio, electricity, the telephone, the world wars, the cell phone, the internet, all shown in rapid flashes…"

Medium 0103 pointed out that the spirit world guides humanity on an individual basis, with inspirations that are often mistaken for random ideas, stating that notable historical figures like Thomas Edison were guided by the spirit, leading to advancements that improve human life and spiritual progress, "Thomas Edison would sit and hold something in his hand until they got into sort of the hypnogogic state and when the ball dropped out of his hand, he would open his eyes. But it was in that in-between state; perhaps that's meditation for you. And it was that for him where the light bulbs literally went off his head. He was inspired. The word inspire means something in spirit is coming through. It's not from ourselves…"

Expanding on this, Medium 0109 affirmed, "We have sent you messengers, inspired with vision and love. Some are your scientists; some are your religious leaders. Edison, Crooke, Einstein. Your scientists have peeled away the layers of illusion so that you can clearly see that this world is an illusion, one created just for you to learn to love. We touch you in dreams. We whisper in your ear. We send leaders to inspire you. The Dalai Lama. Billy Graham. And you have heard. Look around you. Your technology allows you to explore the world and connects you with everyone, even in remote crevices. You are outraged at injustices you find that once were accepted. Your battles are not to survive but to thrive."

Regarding Tesla, Medium 0110 explained that he "was inspired by The Other Side and interdimensional beings to create inventions which improved Humanity's standard of living and comfort. Just having lights at night leads to more freedom, communication, and socialization, which in turn leads to spiritual progress. Having abundant electricity, in turn, led to hundreds of other inventions that led to humankind's spiritual progress. And these inventions were also inspired by The Other Side in many cases."

Medium 0101 said, "They teach us new things, they give us new technology, they teach us how to connect through telepathy, and how to access that frequency." This same medium also mentioned that "new technology will help us to connect to God, help us to be centered, a way to connect Him and Himself, and, more importantly, that we are not focused on multiple religions."

Similarly, Medium 0102 claimed, "We have been in a dark age of spiritual progress, but we are now coming out of that, and both interdimensional beings (IDB) and spirits will be around more. We will be moving forward using technology."

Also referring to the Other Side's influence on new technology development, Medium 0103 stated that "there's been a development in people opening up more because they're starting to seek answers. They're starting to look for things; they're starting to research things. Having technology makes it a lot easier to research (ideas). So, the more research, the more technology you have, or the easier it is for you to get that information, the easier it's for you to understand and learn how to use it and open up more."

In sum, the spiritual world seems to be tightly connected with technological and scientific advancements. After all, as Medium 2007 pointed out, "The technology, CC, the all-knowing manufactured, the knowing comes from the soul." (The monitor is called "CC" by her grandchildren, something that the medium would have no way of knowing.)

As Medium 0110 claimed, this even includes "the proliferation of the near-death experiences in the past many years, which have occurred because of advances in medical technology. (Inspired by TOS) This has led to considerable wisdom acquisition for all Humanity."

The following specific examples were given. These were often presented to the mediums in symbolic form: For example, when given the number for question 3, medium 0114 immediately drew the benzene ring; this medium has only a high school education and, out of trance, denied knowing anything of chemistry.

Planet Earth: When presented with the respective number, one medium said she was being shown a vision of giant hands moving towards and away from each other in a rhythmic pattern and the Earth appearing.

Death as spiritual progress: When presented with the number linked to Question 2, several mediums said "death." One entity continued, "Death is a time for rest, for reflection."

Ice Age: The Ice Age changed the way that humans progressed towards the ultimate goal of the Universe. Humanity had to move around the Earth, discover new ideas, work together for survival, and find their place as one people, one humanity.

Iron Age: The technology of the Iron Age led to religion.

(ISSC note: This vision was presented to Medium in 2005. She did not understand it. It is worth mentioning that Iron Age technology directly led to humans having a centralized government with a distinct ruling class, for example, the rise of the Persian empires, as steel weapons were superior to bronze or stone weapons. Towards the end of the Iron Age, the Axial Age began, the birth of the major religions.)(Armstrong K 2006)

Religion: Religion was supposed to help humans find wisdom within, but they transformed it into something different. Humans got in the way and changed the answers. They failed the test of religion (as it was initially presented).

Ten Commandments: The stone tablets of the Ten Commandments represent a significant milestone in human spiritual development.

Jesus: Jesus was a prophet, brought to earth to advance Mankind.

Inspirational leaders: TOS has sent messengers inspired by vision and love, leaders to inspire us, including the Dalai Lama, Billy Graham, Martin Luther King Jr., and others.

Inspired inventions: The radio, the telephone, the cell phone, the internet, and many other inventions were inspired by Spirit. Edison, Crooke, Einstein, and Tesla are examples. Lesser-known examples include inspiration through dreams and the development of technology, such as magnetic propulsion and the ability to stop time.

Social Movements: The spirit world influenced the Civil Rights movement and inspired key figures like Martin Luther King Jr.

Blood circulation: When asked the third BICS question, Medium 0006 replied: "I am being shown something about blood. How it circulated. (Note: The entity may have been referring to William Harvey, who discovered the circulation of blood, which triggered the scientific advances of the Enlightenment. He credited his discoveries to divine inspiration.)

Sidewalks: Spirit is credited with even the development of sidewalks, which were first used a millennium or two after the invention of the wheel and popularized in heavily traveled city streets in the 19th century. The sidewalks of Paris specifically occurred after 1867.

Vaccine Development: There is a mention of Nicholas Tesla and Jonas Salk, suggesting that while humans developed the Salk vaccine, such advancements might have been inspired by spiritual or otherworldly sources (Salk and Tesla have said that interdimensional beings or aliens gave them ideas)

Near-Death Experiences: Advances in medical technology have led to an increase in near-death experiences, which in turn have contributed to humanity's considerable acquisition of wisdom.

Advancements in Medical Technology: The spirit world has contributed to medical technology, leading to longer, healthier lives for humanity. This includes advancements across various fields of medicine.

Ocular surgery: Various medical procedures on the eye were also said to be inspired by TOS.

Transplant Technology: The mediums speak of transplant technology as a significant medical advancement inspired by the spirit world, contributing to Mankind's good.

Discovery of Blood Types: TOS is said to have led to the discovery of different blood types in 1900, a crucial advancement in medical science.

Future Spiritual Discovery: Mediums also predicted a future discovery that will significantly accelerate human spiritual development and bring a new level of consciousness about Earth's unique position in the Universe.

C2.- What Allan Kardec Said

"When certain discoveries' proper time has come, the spirits in charge of directing progress search for the appropriate persons to accomplish them, inspiring them with the necessary ideas but leaving them all the merit because they will have to develop the ideas and carry them out. This is the process for all the great works of human intelligence."

"The Mediums Book" Chapter XXVI. p. 410

C3.- Role of Death In Spiritual Progress:

The core mediums also emphasized the connection between spiritual progress and the concept of Death. They suggested that understanding and accepting Death as a natural and not fearful part of life is crucial for spiritual growth and that Death is a transformative experience that leads to spiritual advancement:

After being asked what TOS is doing to evolve us, Medium 0110's entity said, "Death and suffering are necessary for human evolution."

Medium 0001 affirmed that Death is part of spiritual progress. Transition back and forth, from life to the Other Side and back, is one way of spiritual progress. This coincides almost precisely with what Medium 0102 stated, "Death also plays a role in spiritual evolution. After humans die, they become closer to The I AM and can communicate with him, improving communication with the living."

As Medium 0001 explained, expanding on the topic:

"Do not fear Death; it is the great engine of spirituality. Death and life are parallel. I see parallel lines. I see birds migrating. Death and life are like a great migration. We fly as a group to other grounds, to another place. All parts of us."

Viewed from this perspective, Death is not and cannot be considered the end. As Medium 0116 explained, "Everything happens for us to learn from it. There is no death, so why do you say that war and Death are a horror? You will see that it is all gain; no one really dies or loses anything."

Medium 2005 expressed that even "911 was given to us to help us spiritually." This statement caused the medium extreme distress as the medium disagreed with and didn't understand this answer. The entity showed the medium "something about nursing, medical, integrating medicine." The medium was confused and distressed but then somewhat calmed down after being shown the vision concerning nursing and medicine.

When asked by the monitor if recent wars, which cause so much death, have created chaos for the Other Side, Medium 0116 explained, "Everything happens for us to learn from it. There is no death, so why do you say that war and Death is a horror? You will see that it is all gain; no one really dies or loses anything (…) "There is no death. No one gets killed in reality."

Medium 0102 added, "Often tragedies create spiritual progress by bringing people together. Examples of this are the Oklahoma City bombings and Jonestown. These were created by the I AM, specifically to advance human progress."

Medium 0115's entity defined death as "one of the greatest processes of growth. It is a part of living to give your Spirit a chance to rest so that you can reflect on that which happened in your lifetime. Understand that it's only about love."

Medium 0102's entity explained, "Death also plays a role in spiritual evolution. After humans die, they become closer to The I AM and can communicate with him, resulting in improved communication with the living."

C4.- What Allan Kardec Said:

154. Frequently, the body suffers more during life than at the moment of death; the soul itself feels nothing at death. The suffering that is sometimes experienced at the moment of death is pleasure for the spirit, for it sees that the end of its exile is at hand." (Kardec, 2006, p. 153).

"In each new life, a spirit takes another step on the path of progress. When it has stripped itself of all impurities; it has no further need of the trials of corporeal life" (Kardec, 2006, p. 162).

D.- BICS Question Four: Answers

The following analysis considers the answers given by the mediums to the fourth question:

"To what extent have earthbound spirits since 1857 impeded, sabotaged, or distorted the progress of human spiritual evolution?"

Medium 0116 entity's response was: "Spirits cannot harm humans. Humans harm themselves. Nevertheless, they evolve due to their mistakes and only by falling you can rise. (Monitor) "Well, can you give an example? Is war an example?" (Entity) War fever mistakes takes heartbreak. They all serve to make people grow. Think of how wars that took place long ago helped to unite people and learn that these are part of a way of primitive behavior that has to occur just like a mistake that needs to be overcome without mistakes, without fear, without wars, man cannot evolve."

Medium 2003's entity agreed, saying: "No one is holding it back; humans are responsible for their own lack of progress."

Before analyzing these answers further, it is advisable to determine what the mediums define as "earthbound spirits." The term "earthbound spirits" describes a host of entities. Medium 0110 even stated: "This is a difficult question because it is my supposition that there are no earthbound spirits, but rather that those beings that are seen as earthbound spirits are actually bleed over from other dimension."

D1.- Defining Earthbound Spirits and Their Role

Medium 0115's entity stated: "The Earthbound spirit is a soul who has chosen to incarnate in order to progress in its soul's journey to ultimately return to the one. And this is a place in which earthbound spirits can work to fully understand it's not just about humanity. This is one of many, many worlds and it is one world in which spirits can or souls to use one of your terms, go to school to learn."

Most mediums suggested that earthbound spirits are individual entities belonging to the spiritual realm, possessing positive and negative influences on human spiritual evolution. As they described, these spirits play a complex role in shaping humankind's spiritual journey, offering guidance, presenting challenges, and sometimes acting as catalysts for growth and reflection.

Upon receiving the Fourth BICS Question's corresponding number, the entity contacted by Medium 0001 said earthbound spirits "are necessary to progress (…) even the sabotage is progress."

Medium 0114's entity described them as those (spirits) that cannot leave this dimension. "It is a spirit that cannot leave Earth; its feet are planted in dirt," adding that some guide and advise humans to stop harming each other and heal themselves. "Some guide you, some tell you what to do and where to go…"

Regarding their nature or essence, Medium 0102 said "They are what we otherwise call ghosts."

Medium 2003's entity said, "Earthbound spirits are spirits who chose to stay. They are here to help us, connect with us."

Medium 2004's entity affirmed, "People project their own fear and call it an evil spirit or earthbound spirit as they are not willing to take responsibility for their own choice."

Medium 2002's added that these spirits are "entities of the universe who just like the duality on earth," and "have interest in not holding a higher vibration for those on earth. They're energy vampires, they feed off of chaos, of negative energies, turmoil and all the things that are, it's very easy for them to create that atmosphere here on earth to feed off of it, to feed off of that energy."

Medium 0103's said "Earthbound spirits are often spirits who have a strong connection to humans. This can be positive or negative."

Medium 0106's stated "Earthbound spirits that we experience are mostly bleed-overs from extra dimensions... These extradimensional beings we often wrongly perceive as earthbound spirits are often here to help us."

Medium 0103 defines these entities as spirits with a solid connection to humans, which can be both positive and negative. An example given is of a spirit comforting a living relative. "Chris feels very close to his grandfather, and his grandfather remains here on Earth to comfort him." This quote highlights the positive influence of earthbound spirits in providing comfort and support to the living.

In this interchange, the entity was referring to the medium. This shows the complexity of the medium's relationship with the entities. Chris is a psychic medium, yet this comment was directly channeled through him from the entity; he went into a brief trance when receiving this message.

According to Medium 0106, earthbound spirits are fallen ones who hold back human progress, alongside bad humans who no longer listen and believe lies. Regarding their origin and nature, the same medium stated, "Earthbound spirits that we experience are mostly bleed-overs from extra dimensions... These extradimensional beings we often wrongly perceive as earthbound spirits are often here to help us."

Highlighting their ultimate purpose in learning and evolution, Medium 0116 described earthbound spirits as souls on a learning journey. "The Earthbound spirit is a soul who has chosen to incarnate in order to progress in its soul's journey to ultimately return to The One...".

Most mediums portrayed earthbound spirits as entities with both positive and negative influences on human spiritual evolution. They depicted them as essential components of the spiritual ecosystem, playing varied roles in guiding, teaching, and even challenging humans on their spiritual journeys.

D2.- Negative Influence of These Spirits

The entity contacted by Medium 0106 stated that earthbound spirits "hold back human progress (...) they sabotage, they destroy, they harm."

Medium 0101's entity said, "These are evil beings or spirits that are not connected to God," and likewise said they "are holding us back."

Medium 0102's entity affirmed, "bad humans and bad spirits are significantly impeding human progress; it may be that the concept of 'bad human' or 'bad spirit' is holding us back, as much as the actual 'bad' part of it." Yet, there clearly is a role for bad humans/spirits in preventing progress. For example, while a person was alive, with free will, he may have done bad things by choice. After he dies, he is still angry and still earthbound and can cause problems such as making others angry. However, this angry Spirit can change, can repent and reflect on what he has done wrong and progress to no longer being earthbound."

Medium 0102 also mentioned there are at least two sets of interdimensional beings (IDB) inhabit this Earth currently and are hidden from humanity. They are actively trying to destroy both humanity and the Earth, through a variety of ways. There are IDBs who exist in another dimension and are also actively sabotaging humanity. But a second interdimensional race is interested in humanity. We often perceive them as angels. They are not as yet involved; they are watching from afar."

Medium 0113's entity stated: "Yes, they are preventing people from evolving and they are preventing people from opening their mind and waking up. Really. They're the ones that are making men crazy and making 'em go to the war and make 'em hate each other. Not only men, but women too. And they're lacking or causing people to lack empathy."

Again and again, the entities stress that earthbound spirits can only sabotage or impede through their actions on humans, not on their own.

D3.- Positive Influence of These Spirits

As Medium 001 claimed, most mediums also state that earthbound spirits are necessary for the soul's journey and learning process, playing a complex role in the broader context of spiritual development.

The Spirit contacted by Medium 0001 affirmed that "There is a network of information that is woven into the fabric of the Universe, and this network of information is linked to us through space and time by the continuity of chaos and life creation throughout the Universe. Our job is to focus on not breaking the chain of connection, not breaking the network."

Similarly, both mediums 0102 and 0115 view earthbound spirits as integral to human spiritual communication and growth, with a role in balancing and fostering progress.

As Medium 0115 explained, "It is part of how the world is made up that there are counterbalances in your world. So there has to be a balance of a weight on the other side for people to grow to realize if people are just good all the time, what you call good loving one another, taking care of each other, it does not help the soul to grow, to progress, to do what needs to be done so they can move on."

When the monitor asked Medium 0115 if earthbound spirits were fostering spiritual progress by impeding and sabotaging progress, the reply was, "Absolutely. It's part of how the world is set up. All we hope is that there will be more who are open to receiving and being a part of making the human experience a more powerful one for the journey of love."

These quotes collectively illustrate the entities' belief in the essential role of positive and negative forces in spiritual evolution. They depict a dynamic spiritual realm where challenges, presented by both beneficial and malevolent spiritual entities, are necessary for human growth and understanding.

To all the above, Medium 2006's entity added, "I want to make it very clear that everything comes from love and light. Right here. They're telling me, sorry. They're telling me they were with us before we got here, and they're with us now." This same medium also stated that the spirit world attempts to contact individuals multiple times daily.

Medium 0110 was asked if these entities, which according to her are "bleedovers" from another dimension, are sabotaging our progress stated "No. In most cases, bleed over from other dimension is to teach you a lesson that you've learned elsewhere that you want to remember in this reality."

D4.- Human Choices and Free Will:

Many mediums emphasize the significant role of human decisions and actions in shaping spiritual progress. The idea is that humans, through their choices, can either advance or impede their spiritual development.

As Medium 0110's entity stated: "we misunderstand what our earthbound spirits, uh, and I, you know, I i, that there's really, there's many people walking on many rocks that, uh, are, are intersecting in intermittent dimensional ways. And sometimes they come near us that by and large, however, that what we call spirits are out there to do us good and not bad. But nevertheless, um, our spiritual evolution is impeded perhaps by 60 to 70%, but mostly because of our education and our own limitations. The way to correct this is to create more roots. And the proper way to find out these roots is to simply live life."

As Medium 0114 entity's stated, "We haven't made much progress, but earthbound spirits are not impeding, distorting or sabotaging the progress; it is rather a lack of understanding by humans. Yes. Yes. The understanding is the key."

The entity contacted by Medium 0102 stated that it is "because of free will that He (The I Am) watches, but often doesn't intervene... Bad is a gradient; there is no true bad or good; it is just people with different agendas.".

Medium 2004's entity, upon recognizing the importance of free will, sustained, "The great news is you can change your mind at any point because you have free will. You can choose to go down that path if you want to, and you can choose another way. We do not judge or condemn you for either choice; however, we want you to connect with us. It's way more fun that way."

Medium 0110's entity declared, "We humans often make our own choices, which creates a lifepath that is a hellish one, which leads to a distortion of spiritual progress," while Medium 0115 added, "The nature of the world is so you can choose. It is designed so that human beings can progress in their souls and their spirits. And that requires challenging temptation, bad things happening what you call bad. So, it's not a matter of winning or losing. It is a matter of it's all there together, and it's essential for the human journey."

Regarding free will, Medium 0110 declared, "Bad humans are much of the problem; earthbound spirits are not that much of a problem. We continue to teach our children wrong methods and inaccurate ways of handling problems. Bad people are the result of bad training…" He also added, "We humans often make our own choices, which creates a lifepath that is a hellish one, which leads to a distortion of spiritual progress."

These quotes collectively illustrate the mediums' understanding that human choices and free will are fundamental to spiritual development. They emphasize the power of individual actions and decisions in influencing one's spiritual path, as well as the broader spiritual evolution of humanity.

D5. What Allan Kardec Said

"They are often unhappy due to their own fault and for having disregarded the voice that warned them in their conscience, and God allows them to suffer the consequences so that they may serve as a lesson for the future." (Kardec, 1987, p. 375)

"By giving humans free will, God wanted them to reach the point where, through their own experience, they could distinguish between good and evil, and that the practice of the good be the result of their own efforts and will." (Kardec, 1987, p. 269)

D6.- Communication With the Other Side

There is a recurring emphasis on the importance of establishing and maintaining a positive interconnection with the spiritual realm. This includes the idea that humans must be more receptive to guidance and messages from spirits or other entities to aid their spiritual journey.

Medium 0102 indicates, "Earthbound spirits play a positive role. They are connected to the spirit world, and they are an easier means for humans to communicate with The Other Side.

According to Medium 0110, lack of communication with the spirit world is part of the problem, "He says that humans themselves are holding themselves back by not having empathy for others, by not choosing love, by not learning and communicating with each other, especially people we don't understand or like. We also ignore the input from our guides, some of whom are interdimensional guides in addition to spirit guides. We don't know that we can ask them for help, and we ignore the help they try to give us."

Explaining the importance of universal interconnectivity, Medium 001 explained, "I see a gigantic array of threads all held in the middle by a pin, and the medium it is in starts pivoting as such that all threads start turning like branches of a galaxy. I am told that those threads are the threads of life and they revolve around the center. But what moves is not them but the medium they are in. And all the threads can do is to follow the movement, the circular movement until a full spiral has been created. Humanity has to revolve the same way around the center of higher achievement, but there it is, revolving in a medium that creates the movement. And that medium is the great unknown. If we find the medium, we find the solution."

D7.- What Allan Kardec Said

"Spirit communications with humans are either concealed or direct. Concealed communications – undetectable in a physical sense – occur through the good or bad influence they exert on us without our even suspecting it, and it depends on our own judgment to distinguish between their good and bad inspirations." (Kardec, 2006, p. 43)

Table 2: The Mediums Answers to the Questions

Medium Number	Medium Type	Answer to Question 1A (Lack of progress)	Answer to Question 1B (Who is winning)	Answer to Question 4 (to what extent have earthbound spirits impeded progress)	Who is Impeding Progress?	Who is to Blame for Lack of Progress
0106	Trance	Yes	Bad humans	No	Humans, especially liars	Humans
0110	Trance	Yes	Both	No	Humans not choosing love	Humans
2007	Trance	Undetermined		No	No one	No one
0102	Mental	No		No	No one	No one
0112	Mental	Yes	Bad humans	No	Humans who are afraid	Humans
0113	Mental	Yes	Bad humans	No	Bad spirits that affect humans	Humans
0114	Mental	No	Spirits are helping	No	Humans who stay quiet	Humans
0115	Mental	No		No	No One	No One
0116	Mental	Yes	No one	Undetermined	Undetermined	Humans

0117	Mental	Yes	No one	No	No one	Humans
2004	Mental/trance	No		No	Humans who project fear	Humans
2005	Mental	Yes	No one	Undetermined		Humans
2006	Psychic	Yes	Fear	Moderate	Humans who are afraid	Humans
0101	Psychic	Undetermined	No one	Moderate	Spirit world's effects on humans	Humans
0103	Psychic	Undetermined		Moderate	Spirit world's effects on humans	Humans
0108	Psychic	Yes	No one	Moderate	Humans who hate	Humans
0109	Psychic	Yes	No one	Undetermined		Humans
2002	Psychic	Yes	No one	Significantly	Spirits who feed on chaos	Humans
2003	Psychic	No	No one	No	No One	Humans who fear

E.- Importance of the BICS Project

"What he (Bigelow) is seeking is also seeking him."

The Other Side was asked to address the issue of humanity's failure to progress spiritually since the time of Allan Kardec and who is to blame for that failure. They clearly state that humans are to blame. They portray themselves as active participants in this inquiry, stating at the project's onset that they inspired the questions and BICS to ask them. So, it is unsurprising to learn that they have a personal message for BICS, which the ISSC team would be remiss in not including in this presentation.

After Medium 0114 contacted a group of "intelligent bubbles," she asked how TOS has helped humanity, and the bubbles responded: "Open communication between us and you, what's in the bubble (The Other Side) and what's outside the bubble." The medium said, "They telepathically communicate to us and we are not to take everything literally. I think that was my interpretation. Yeah. Well, that's important because clearly this (comment) is being aimed at you (BICS)."

When asked whether TOS helps individual people or groups of people, Medium 0106's entity replied: "Groups and individual. I put people where they need to be to do my job, to get the answers. I put them where they need to be. Your project (BICS) has (what) it needs to have. You know I Am The I Am. You know, I put them there."

Regarding Bigelow's role, the entity contacted by Medium 0106 affirmed: "With his (Bigelow's) money, he can remove the saboteurs. He will know when it's time. I will make sure he will know through you (ISSC). I will make sure you know through you. Be careful, liars. Be careful. Liars, snakes. You cut the snakes at the head. Do not let the liars do not let the liars. He (Bigelow) dreams the real. He dreams the real. Dreams. Dreams the real. When I give him messages through the dream, I give him all the answers through the dream. He (again, Bigelow) knows the crafts. He knows what the Universe holds. He knows the universal."

Medium 2004 stated: "They're really, really happy for this research and these questions, and it's part of this awakening and the spiritualness because more people will hear about things. It plants the seeds for them."

Regarding the BICS role, Medium 0116's entity sustained that "Mr. Bigelow should continue his path of understanding that there is a veil of lies (in this reality) and misunderstandings of what he calls the spiritual side and should prepare himself for more forming discoveries and experiences to prove that what he is seeking is also seeking him."

Medium 0113's entity spoke of a key that represents humanity's ability to progress spiritually. It currently is hidden, or many people have parts of it. The key, which appears to be a metaphor for wisdom, is associated, according to the entity with BICS: "The Bigelow Institute. I think he's already got a good start trying to show that we're (TOS) supporting the idea that this is a little bit bigger than you, me, anybody out there. So, he is trying to prove that we are kind of all from one consciousness. Well, I don't know if Mr. Bigelow is trying to do that. Still, he is on a course to study our separateness and why we (humans) feel we are separate with obviously me (the entity), I (the entity) feel connected to everything and everybody around me, but a lot of humans don't. So he (Mr. Bigelow) is doing things to taking steps and he is on the right path for whatever he's got next."

This dialogue demonstrates the mangled syntax that often occurs with mental mediums as they try to navigate bilocation as they speak to and for both the entity and the monitor.

Medium 0114 directly contacted Allan Kardec's spirit, as described in the Supplemental questions presented in the Appendix.

This is unequivocal proof that Kardec's spirit was obtained. It was clear that Kardec purposely provided this information, which cannot be found in any public sources and is only known to two individuals as a very private matter, to emphasize his opinion as to the importance of this project.

V.- Discussion

As scientists, the ISSC team prepared to analyze the results from a statistical point of view, anticipating that there would be a wide range of responses and that these would have to be analyzed to find commonalities and prevailing themes. Surprisingly, when the team took a different tack and treated the mediums' responses as one long, disjointed conversation with The Other Side, all the contradictions and seeming confusions in the responses were suddenly cleared up.

The first attempt was to identify commonalities in each medium's responses to look for statistically significant patterns. The team used a variety of approaches, including scatter plots and bubble charts, to look for correlations. The team then tried reducing the information to binary units, which can be further analyzed statistically. None of these approaches helped the team better understand the data.

The transcripts from the first and last interviews were then organized chronologically. This resulted in a robust understanding of the material and, most importantly, organized all the data into a coherent whole without having to exclude anything, which would have been the case from a statistical approach.

The team had been informed through the entities repeatedly that they spoke with one voice through the various mediums' language and cultural understandings. Their message was clearly understood when that approach was taken.

When test Medium 0001's responses were added to the timeline, it was suddenly understood that her session was actually the first statement from TOS concerning the questions, so her answers have been included in the Results section.

Question 1: Assessed as one Long Conversation with Tos

1. Since 1857, has the Other Side failed, and Mankind failed to achieve good progress in securing human spirituality? If so, are bad spirits and bad humans winning?

The conversation began even before the formal project began when the team first tested the protocol with Medium 0001.

The entity she contacted immediately stated that humanity has failed and that humans are to blame.

Medium 0102 attempts to clarify the answer. After 0001's firm statement that humanity is at fault, TOS now tries to blunt that message. TOS now states that the spirit world has failed, just as a school or parent fails when a student or child fails. TOS discusses that because humanity is not progressing in an easy-to-document and understandable manner does not mean bad spirits and humans are "winning."

Through Medium 0106, TOS continues to try to explain what seems contradictory: just because humans have not progressed according to their potential doesn't mean they have failed. She presents the image of the roller coaster and states, "We are on a mission, a mission (to learn) to love."

Then, TOS, through Medium 1009, introduces the idea that this reality is transitional; he is shown a vision of a gateway or portal indicating how to enter and leave this reality to pass on to others.

Through medium 1010, the TOS addresses the lack of progress. They point out it has only been 167-plus years since Allan Kardec, and they tend to take a one-thousand view of humanity.

Also, through Medium 1010, TOS points out that humanity has made fantastic progress in the time period in question. Women and persons of color have the vote. Hundreds of thousands of young men lost their lives in the Civil War, giving their lives to get rid of slavery. TOS mentions an endless stream of prophets, such as Sojourner, Swedenborg, and Martin Luther King Jr. One medium when interviewing Allan Kardec on this point saw a rapid slide show of all the advances humanity has made in recent years. The implication is that even though humans appear to have failed in human spiritual progress, given what is happening today, they must reflect that even the partial progress has been remarkable.

Medium 0113 now addresses the issue of why humanity has not progressed

For the first time, TOS raises the issue of free will. This was also presented through Medium 1010 (both interviews were in the same time period), who stated that TOS prefers not to be involved but to let humans "Mindstorm" their problems.

Now, through Mediums 0113 and 0115, TOS emphasizes its limited role in preventing humans from making bad choices. Humans need to acknowledge the responsibilities of free will. There is a clear statement that they can inspire people but have limited means of preventing them from stupid mistakes such as self-extinction.

Yet still, the message is that it is grim but not too late. Through love and recognition of free will, humanity can avert disaster, but the fact that no one will save them is established.

Next was Medium 0101, a psychic medium guided by voices within, spiritual guides, and intuition. His contribution was a detailed description of the current, ongoing battle. All the mediums acknowledged it was happening, yet Medium 0101 described in detail the various interdimensional beings, angels, spirit guides, and other intelligent entities as they fought to win this spiritual war.

Now comes Medium 0103. He points out that humans have had periods of great spiritual awakening since 1857 and references the many prominent scientists who worked with mediums in the late 1800s in England and the United States. He points out that the veil between TOS is getting thinner, and energy is shifting. During this same time period, the team heard from several mediums. The current BICS was described as a continuation of the scientific investigations of mediumship in the late 1800s, implying that this should continue.

Medium 0108 was next: She now elevates the conversation to a higher level. Speaking through her, the TOS acknowledges that humanity has failed and identifies the main reason: the spirit world tries to help humans, but they often will not listen. They now state that there are many paranormal tools that humans are not using that would connect them with the spirit world, but again, since many don't believe in The Other Side, there is no interest in developing these tools.

Next, TOS clarified why some mediums had encouraging messages and others warning of disaster. Medium 0114 was told that humanity is on a balance beam with life-threatening dangers on either side. Some entities encourage people to do it, yet others emphasize the dangers and warn them.

Medium 0116 now states that humanity has failed because they do not listen to TOS. However, TOS now introduces a new concept: Failure to progress spiritually is an expected part of human spiritual evolution. So, although perhaps humans are failing, it is not a race but more like levels in a video game. There are lessons of love that people must learn, and they can learn at their own pace.

The conversation now moved to the Charleston mediums. TOS once again demonstrated that the questions could be answered when presented as numbers, which validated ISSC's protocol. However, once they established that they knew the questions, they did not repeat the previous answers but continued expanding on their message.

Through the Charleston mediums, TOS wanted to encourage humans as they struggled with these difficult times. They said not to fear the upheaval to come, as it is necessary before change occurs.

So, the first 13 interviews were to clearly warn the team members about possible catastrophic events leading to extinction. Now, they are reassured that upheaval can lead to the positive transformation of societies.

Medium 2002 explains the complex relationship between humans and spirits. Humans are not separate from the spirit world. As people evolve, they evolve.

Again, they said that Spirit World had initiated this project. They formed the questions, inspired the mediums, and ensured BICS hired the proper teams.

Medium 2003 message was also of encouragement. She was invited to eat dinner with St. James, who stated: Progress has been made; it doesn't make sense to stop and turn around. Stop judging yourself that you should be further ahead. Failure is fear; stop your fear with love.

For the first time, they state that the answer is within people. They need to start trusting themselves; others do not need to answer these questions; people know the answers and must act.

St. James says that humans and the spirit world are connected because spirits can feel emotions with them and share their love or anger. Spirits don't put these emotions in people's heads, but when people do something kind or loving for someone, they share in the experience.

Medium 2004 was the last to answer Question 1 directly. This now is a final pep talk,

"No, the answer is no. (to question 1). you are loved beyond measure. There's nothing to fear. No need to fear. You are safe despite the fact that your body tells you otherwise. Sometimes, we are inspired by your determination nation, and we're sending you signs all the time and signals so that you know you are safe and it's all organized; it's done. More say there's A feeling of just joy and expansion and love and a little bit of, come on, you guys, we've got this. We're cheering you on. We know you've got this.

"We're here giving you guys guidance every day, every minute. Unfortunately, some of you are caught up in the day-to-day physical, and you forget to stop and connect to love, which is us. We are here. We have not failed. No one has failed. Keep going."

Questions 2 and 3: A Timeline of the Answers

2. Explain to people on Earth why the Other Side has not failed in fostering spiritual evolution.

3. What difference has the Other Side made in the past 166 years in influencing humans to accelerate their spiritual progress?

Question two asks what TOS has done in the past to help humanity progress in spirituality. Question 3 is essentially the same question but asks, "What have you done for us lately?" TOS typically answered both questions at the same time.

Once again, reading the answers from the first interview to the last revealed a robust, comprehensive answer that begins with an opening statement, presents evidence through subsequent interviews, and ends with a powerful closing statement.

Medium 0001: TOS firmly states that humanity is making spiritual progress. The spirit world is a higher order, and people cannot understand how it shapes them. This is an essential introductory statement by TOS, as BICS has asked that these two questions be answered as if they were presented in a Court of Law. BICS wanted evidence, not platitudes.

This first piece of evidence seems like a platitude until humans understand the science of the relationship between TOS and this reality. As the ISSC team presents in the Additional Background and Context Section, there is considerable scientific theory and evidence to validate the concept of immaterial forces such as mathematics shaping physical reality. TOS is an immaterial force; its precise structure is as yet unknown. However, solid scientific evidence shows that material forces are influenced by the immaterial.

So, this initial statement mediated through Medium 1001 could be considered TOS's opening statement to the jury.

TOS's Opening Statement to the BICS Jury

Our assessment of TOS's opening statement is, in essence: "Your world was created by us using the mathematical principles your scientists call 'complex systems theory.' By definition, since we are the higher-order process, you cannot understand the rules of reality any more than an amoeba can understand the complex biological system that keeps it alive, or a deer can understand rain. As your medium correctly summarized complex systems theory as it applies to you:

Humanity is like a blob being influenced and shaped by the spirit world. Part of that necessarily involves what we can call 'impediments,' which are really just shaping the blob so it can progress properly. These impediments are caused by a collection of spiritual powers, including Earthbound spirits.

If humans want to understand why they have done poorly in the past 167-plus years, TOS suggests studying the ancient petroglyphs and the Western art of the 12th century. Both periods of time were marked by a profound integration of spirituality and the people's ordinary lives.

Now, TOS addresses an obvious yet frequently overlooked aspect of humanity's spiritual development: death.

One basic structure is that humans will die; an essential part of that dying process is growing spiritually. "This is an often-overlooked primary process because you are so afraid of death."

Even the phrasing of your questions implies that since there are many seemingly meaningless deaths, such as wars, you must fail to progress spiritually. That is an erroneous assumption on your part, which causes you to fail to appreciate the greatest driver of spiritual development in humankind, which is death."

Specifics are Now Given

Medium 0106 and 0113 are now developing this theme. TOS essentially states: "We gave you the Ten Commandments, and you have failed to live up to them. Almost all humans have been exposed to them, yet you ask to prove we have not failed you. Everything you need for spiritual growth was presented thousands of years ago."

"We have worked with your scientists to develop technology to improve your life. Advanced civilization leads to opportunities for spiritual growth as the struggle for survival is no longer all-consuming.

More Examples

The following mediums interviewed, 1009, 1010, 1012, and 1013, presented numerous specific examples of how they have inspired humans, everything from sidewalks to thermometers to songs and religion.

TOS summarizes by pointing out examples of them nudging or directly inspiring individuals. This highlights the importance of faith, especially in scientists. If William Harvey had not faith in God, he would never have been inspired to find God's immaterial processes inherent in the rules of the natural world.

Remedies

TOS uses these questions not only to illustrate humanity's failures but also to present remedies.

Medium 0112 discusses the need and uses of "light workers." This is an excellent example of how this is all one dialogue, as she is picking up on a previous medium's metaphor of lanterns, which are ideas from the spirit world that humans must pick up. Lightworkers are open to inspiration from the spirit world, see what has to be done, and then do it. The world needs more light workers.

Robert Bigelow is specifically mentioned as a light worker who knows what needs to be done. Medium 1006 urged him to trust his BICS challenge grant recipients, his dreams, and his instincts as they (TOS) are working with his grant recipients and directly with him.

TOS emphasizes that these lightworkers are often found in communities, the working class, and ordinary citizens but are not usually seen in politicians or those entrusted with power.

Through Medium 0112, the TOS acknowledges that humanity has gone backward in the past 167 years.

She states:

"I'm getting the, you can lead a horse to water. They give us the tools. We've shunned information. We've turned our nose up at information out of fear and ego and what we deem as unimportant."

Medium 0102 amplifies this message. He adds that not only the Spirit World has helped but also interdimensional beings. He adds more about the composition of the spirit world. He restates the troublesome examples of TOS efforts to promote spirituality (troublesome to us), which involve their involvement in catastrophes such as the Oklahoma City bombing. People cannot reject the idea that the Jonestown suicide was divinely inspired simply because it caused mass death. Death is an engine of spiritual growth.

The I Am addresses the issue of whether or not he has failed humanity.

He states, "Mankind has (recently) resisted my efforts. They no longer believe in me; they believe in lies about me."

The implication is that the remedies for humanity's lack of progress are to have greater faith in God, stop resisting spiritual guidance, and look beyond the death associated with world events to see the spiritual growth associated with them.

Next: More Advanced Concepts

TOS through medium 1016 explains that humanity and the spirit world are inextricably linked. Humans think they are different because they can't see the connection. TOS uses the example of hands and feet. They have different roles, are seemingly disconnected if you can't see the body, and are one entity. So, humanity's failure is the spirit world's failure. Now the team can understand why the mediums, while answering the BICS question, some picked up on the sense of failure, and others the sense of success. It is all one process. Humans evolve with the spirit world. There is no separation between the two.

Medium 0116 came back to the issue of wars. Since BICS wanted answers that would stand up in a Court of Law, the monitor expressed frank disbelief at this concept and directly asked, "So you are saying that the horrors of Gaza are inspired and approved of by the Spirit World?

The answer from TOS was a firm "YES." At this point, TOS expressed irritation and frustration that humans could not understand this. He stated, "Why are you so afraid of death? Nothing happens to those who die in Gaza. Their suffering exists, but that is part of their lesson for being here." "Nothing dies."

TOS implies that suffering injustice is an essential lesson of love that humans are here to learn.

This concept that the spirit world engineers wars, suffering, and horrific human events for humanity's spiritual advancement is complicated to understand. Upon transmitting this information, two mediums became visibly distressed, one bursting into tears. Yet it is emphasized repeatedly by TOS, as death is the great engine of spiritual advancement.

What Kardec Said: 784. Humankind's perversity is very great. Doesn't it seem like humans are regressing instead of progressing, at least from a moral point of view? "You are mistaken. Observe the whole closely, and you will see that they are advancing because they have a better understanding of what evil is, leading

them day by day to reform their abuses. The excess of evil will cause them to understand the need for the good and for reforms." (Kardec, 2006, p. 429-

430).

The Other Side's Closing Statement

Medium 2007 is an internationally renowned medium and professor of mediumship. She spoke directly to the monitor in a trance without any input from her own individual consciousness. TOS selected her for the final interview so they could make a statement directly to BICS without distortion from the medium

The Monitor: Can you answer the questions before you? (given as numbers)

Entity: They've been given much thought and are not concerned. Only those who can change. Can change what comes. It is peace that you seek. It is peace you must give. Peace is not on the horizon unless there is a shift. Peace does not have to be far away. It must shift.

Monitor: What do you mean by a shift?

Entity: Choices of love. The choice to not fear, dear. It brings you down. Love brings you up. And that is all. So much worry, so much fear. This can change. This must change. It is not the spirit side that has failed. It's the choices of those in the physical. They choose fear. That's not wisdom. They choose anger. That's not wisdom. They choose pride. That's not wisdom. They choose envy. That's not wisdom. We give love. They must choose the love. They must look through the eyes of the other. They must know that they breathe for one another. They live for one another. They must not kill for one another. This is not love. Touch the land. Feel her heart. Take in her. Knowing the land will tell you much. It has wisdom. The same wisdom is those about the rounds. I cannot tell you the answers you seek. They are inside each of us, each of you and all of us. Oh, with one goal. Love. This is what moves us forward. And yet you fight. Fight for power. Fight for glory.

"We have sent visitors, but many of you choose to ignore them. Your fear makes you find; we have great hopes. We have taught many, and many have responded, but others turn away so afraid. We cannot force you. We cannot force anything. It's not for us to change the world. For those who progress, as you see, it is not always a good thing.

"Can you tell me why we're here on this plane, on this earth? (asks the entity rhetorically) To learn, always to learn. We forget what we know. We must relearn joy. So many opportunities for joy. Forgotten. Ignored, always seeking pain. Pain seems to be a badge of honor. This is not true, though. Joy is the honor.

"We are not stuck. Is this the fear that spirits are stuck? We are not bound to any place, to anywhere. We come with love. We spend time with love. We are not impeded. We do not hurt. We do not bring pain. Only love. Do not be afraid. Your fear is failure. Open your hearts to love."

Question 3 Discussion

To what extent have earthbound spirits since 1857 impeded, sabotaged, or distorted the progress of human spiritual evolution?

Most entities agreed that humanity's spiritual progress has been sabotaged, impeded, and distorted, followed by the emphatic statement that humans are doing it to themselves. When answering the fourth question, most mediums considered the balance between good and evil forces, suggesting that both positive and negative experiences are necessary for spiritual growth. This theme underscores the idea that challenges and adversities are crucial in spiritual learning and evolution. When earthbound spirits are involved, and there are many different types of what are referred to as "earthbound spirits," the comment is invariably that they can only influence humans. Humans can choose to reject the fear, hate, and chaos the spirit world provokes in them.

Question 4 did not benefit from a timeline analysis as it appears to be an encyclopedic presentation of the various types of earthbound spirits and their diverse roles in advancing or hindering human progress. It is a complete presentation from TOS that should be read in its entirety.

What Allan Kardec Said

"Interaction between spirits and humans is constant. Good spirits encourage us to follow the path of the good. They support us in life's trials and help us bear them with courage and resignation. On the other hand, evil spirits encourage us to take the path of evil. It is a pleasure for them when they see us succumb and fall to their level. (Kardec, 2006, p. 43)

99. Are all spirits of the third order altogether evil?

"No, some do neither good nor evil; others, however, take pleasure in evil and are pleased when they find an opportunity for it. Still others are frivolous or foolish spirits, more mischievous than wicked. These take more pleasure in spite than evil, and they also take pleasure in amusing themselves by vexing people and causing them petty annoyances." (Kardec, 2006, p. 124)

VI.- Conclusion

"An urgent call to arms to learn to love, overcome fear, and reject hate."

The coincidences found in the different answers prove that beyond the message conveyed, there seems to be solid evidence of true communication between humans and TOS, something science has not accepted to this date. The BICS project has demonstrated that communication between humans and the spiritual realm is possible and real, allowing this field of research to transition from speculative conceptualizations to hypothesis-generating studies. This leads to fascinating considerations and potential impacts on humanity capable of revolutionizing psychology, neuroscience, and philosophy.

As a direct consequence of the present study, the ISSC team recommends further successive contacts with TOS to bring a deeper understanding of the mysteries surrounding consciousness and its post-mortem persistence. Also worth considering is the possibility of developing new methodologies to allow consistent communication with the spiritual world under controlled conditions, thus making it a part of empirical science. After all, as TOS explained, the future development of technological advancements capable of facilitating this communication is also possible. This could involve advanced AI, quantum computing, or entirely new fields of technology focusing on the interface between physical and spiritual realms.

In any case, proven communication with the spiritual realm can profoundly affect world religions and spiritual beliefs, allowing humans to validate certain beliefs, challenge others, and generally transform humanity's spiritual landscape. The sudden shift from faith to empirical evidence proving the existence of a spiritual could potentially lead to a widespread worldwide transformation.

Using this blinded protocol for presenting the questions, the team found that Spirit World has an urgent message that has been ignored and dismissed since Allan Kardec's time. Willful ignorance and difficulties in spiritual progression have resulted in humanity's current state, where humans could destroy themselves with their unbridled embracement of technology. The Spirit showed how technology can come from a spiritual source and advance humankind's material and spiritual progress.

The underlying subtext to the four questions is that the current world situation of multiple wars, violence, political instability, and the dramatic transformation of the political landscape into warring factions that no longer listen to each other demonstrates a lack of spiritual progress. This current project questions that fundamental assumption, as TOS repeatedly stated, that such conflict is necessary for spiritual development.

TOS emphasized that they encourage people on a personal level and are always available to anyone who needs their comfort, assistance, and guidance. However, they are not responsible for humanity's spiritual progress. Free will and individual choices are the drivers of human spiritual progress. Furthermore, they state that they are far better at inspiring humans, often manipulating humans by putting them in the right place at the right time, than preventing disasters. They gave many examples of encouraging human spiritual growth, from engineering Ice Ages, inspiring technology, sending spiritual messengers, and working with humans on an intimate personal level. They had no examples of preventing world problems or disasters.

For example, TOS gave an example of a young man who suffered a motorcycle accident resulting in his losing an arm and almost drowning. They did nothing to prevent that horrific disaster. However, they did influence several children to play near the accident so that they could witness it and call for help. This was an area that these children did not typically frequent.

When ISSC scientists began this project, they were obligated to present whatever answers they learned through interviewing 19 mediums. The ISSC protocol was designed as the best way to obtain wisdom from TOS but not to filter, influence, or distort whatever messages were received. Here is the best understanding of what the entities are telling BICS through the mediums interviewed:

ISSC's position is that the spirit world inspired this current project to give mankind an urgent message: "Learn to love or be destroyed by your own technology and hate for each other." This is placed in the context that they cannot (or will not) prevent humanity from self-extinction but can warn of impending disaster. Humanity must make the choices necessary to exist as a species; only by making those choices can humanity have the opportunity to continue its spiritual progress.

VII Additional Background and Context

Glossary

NON-LOCAL REALITY: A scientific model of reality begins with theoretical physics and information/complex systems theory. It starts with the understanding that ultimate, or "non-local" reality, is a timeless spaceless electromagnetic field embedded with all the information in the Universe. (Garisto D) (Lohrey A) This reality has at its core mathematical equations that dictate the structure and nature of the physical reality perceived as real. (Theise 2023)

Those who have personally seen and interacted with this non-local reality or domain, such as those who have died and returned to life, tell people that it is conscious and has unconditional love for humanity. (Morse M 1990)(Gaona, J 2022)

LOCAL REALITY: Unlike the timeless, spaceless "non-local" reality, local reality means the shared everyday reality humans exist in and use to interact. Even if they are not essential aspects of ultimate reality, time and space are necessary for human existence as biological systems. (The Encyclopedia of Quantum Physics 2019)

MEDIUMSHIP: ISSC conceptualizes mediumship as human local minds accessing information from this universal information source using existing neuro-perceptual systems, which generate the internal model of shared "local" reality. The medium's mind/brain communicates with the information cluster representing a discarnate entity or universal consciousness; the latter is often called "God."

ISSC recognizes that the term "God" is referenced by various religions, and ISSC is not commenting on which God is authentic but instead uses the term as children who have had NDEs use it when they say they interacted with "God," meaning a loving presence that represents a universal consciousness.

THE OTHER SIDE (TOS): The BICS audience is worldwide, and the mediums represent various American religious and spiritual belief systems. Language is used to be meaningful for all readers. For this reason, non-local reality is sometimes called "The Other Side". At times, the informational universe is conceptualized as consisting of clusters of information representing spirits, discarnate entities, and other conscious aspects of this non-local universe, which contains all of reality.

Terms are used that are broadly understood by the general population as much as possible.

The goal is to use inclusive terminology that will not result in readers rejecting the medium's message because they are uncomfortable with the words humans use.

Yet, the text will always reference the scientific language, which is the essence of understanding new conceptualizations of mediumship resulting from recent advances in neuroscience, mathematics, and the physical sciences.

Research Background

Any study of mediumship begins with the work of Allan Kardec, the renowned French educator. (1804-1869). He owned a school in Paris where he lectured regularly on the physical sciences, including astronomy, chemistry, and physics. He studied mediumship for decades and founded the Spiritist Organization. There are 13 million Spiritists today, primarily physicians, engineers, well-educated individuals, and professionals. Kardec's five books on mediumship form the core principles of their organization. (Spiritist Medical Association). The current project represents an update of Kardec's *Book of the Spirits* and a progress report over the past 167-plus years.

Spiritist scientists and professionals include spiritual realities as part of the material world. For example, Spiritist psychiatric texts consider dissociation (the trance state of a medium) as a potentially healthy and ordinary human experience as opposed to the prevailing Western psychiatric point of view that such dissociation is pathological. (Morse M. 2013)

The Semmelweis Effect: "I Just Don't Believe It"

Kardec's empirical findings conflicted with the materialistic scientific paradigm of the 19th century.

Materialism is the theory that physical matter, consisting of over 100 types of atoms as building blocks, is the only reality and that everything, including thought, feeling, mind, and will, can be explained as byproducts of material reality. (Matter: National Geographic 2024)

When scientists make observations that conflict with the current scientific belief system, they can encounter the "Semmelweis effect" from the scientific community, this is the reflex-like tendency to reject new information if it conflicts with prevailing norms, beliefs, or paradigms. Ignaz Semmelweis was a Viennese physician who discovered in the early 1800s that if he washed his hands before delivering babies, the mothers were less likely to die of childbirth fever. Although he had empiric evidence that handwashing saved lives, it was not until Lister's germ theory presented a mechanism that scientists could believe that "invisible agents" caused disease. (Korzen 2016)

A similar situation exists in consciousness research today. There is considerable experimental evidence that humans can remotely access information through non-ordinary means (Targ, R. 1975, 1980) (Radin D 2008), anticipate immediate future events as demonstrated by changes in blood pressure and heart rate (Bierman, 1997) (McCraty R., 2004), convey emotions and images through telepathy (Montague U 1989), documented cases of children remembering past lives (Tucker J 2007)(Stevenson I., 1980) and even that remote retroactive prayer can heal sepsis (Leibovici L (2001).

These are all documented in peer-reviewed medical and scientific journals such as The Lancet, Nature, and The British Medical Journal, with research done by professors at Cornell University (Bem, 2024), the University of Virginia (Tucker, Stevenson), The University of Nevada Las Vegas (Radin D 1997), and Johns Hopkins. (Powell, D. 2009)

However, it is tough to believe new evidence if there is no reasonable explanation for how it could occur. One scientist declared that the research documenting remote viewing is an average human ability: "I see the evidence; the research is sound. I do not believe it."

Mediumship and the Science of the 21st Century

The premise of this project is that the human mind/brain can contact a discarnate entity, conscious spirit, or soul that exists independent of the mind/brain and can access information from that source to acquire wisdom for the benefit of humanity.

The BICS premise is not an unreasonable presumption, as it is the basis of religious belief systems with resulting personal and cultural behaviors that have existed in all human cultures since the dawn of history. Spiritual and religious behavior linked to specific neurobiological structures have been reported in the medical literature since the 19th century (Saver, 1997). Wilder Penfield, the father of modern neuroscience, with his extensive mapping of the human brain by directly stimulating specific neurobiological sites, reported that deep within the Sylvian fissure of the right temporal lobe were areas when stimulated, patients stated: "Oh God, I am leaving my body," and "I am half in and half out." (Penfield, 1955) Most recently, Neurologist Kevin Nelson presented a comprehensive overview of what he termed "the spiritual doorway" in the brain, which permits spiritual and religious experiences of all kinds. Nelson makes clear that spiritual experiences are not the exception in human life but rather an inescapable and precious part of every one of us. (Nelson 2012)

The neurobiological underpinnings of spirituality address the issue of whether spiritual experiences are hallucinations or inventions of a confused and/or dysfunctional brain. They are associated with the proper functioning of the brain (Morse, 2000). They cannot be considered hallucinations any more than the proper functioning of the occipital cortex would be considered to create hallucinatory visual images.

Matter no Longer Matters

Scientists still speak of "matter," even though many acknowledge that it is an illusion. The fundamental materialistic building block, the atom, is 99.99% empty and is now considered to consist of electrons and quarks, both of which are energetic forms. Indeed, there is no longer a commonly accepted scientific definition of matter. Modern theories of matter indicate that it can be conceptualized as an energetic wave instead of a solid particle. The use of "matter" by scientists today seems to be more of a metaphor than a precise description, as the exact properties of matter so far have eluded modern science. (Britannica.com/matter)

Einstein did not consider this universe to be "real." He stated, "The point mass or the particle *is not a fundamental property* of the physical world. (emphasis added)." Other physicists point out that this universe can only be described using mathematics, meaning that the current scientific model of reality is that unseen immaterial forces shape physical reality. As MIT physics professor Max Tegmark states: The Universe is math. (Tegmark 2014) As Einstein further said: "It appears to me that the "real" is an intrinsically empty, meaningless category, whose monstrous importance lies only in the fact that I can do certain things in it and not certain others. This division is, to be sure, not an *arbitrary* one; I concede that the natural sciences concern the "real," but I am still not a realist." (Howard 2019)

Kuhn Paradigm Shift Cycle Stage 3: Crisis

Thomas Kuhn conceptualizes the scientific paradigm shift as a process of new empirical observations challenging the existing paradigm. First is model drift, followed by crisis, revolution, and finally, acceptance of the new paradigm as "reality" (Kuhn, 1962, pp. 145-56).

ISSC suggests that science is currently in Stage 3 of a paradigm shift, which he defines as the crisis point. This is where experimental and observational data conflict with the reigning paradigm, and new competing theories arise that better explain the new information.

The Science of Mediumship

"Based on our understanding of the natural sciences and current neuroscientific understanding of brain function, we conclude that spirituality, including the existence of a soul, is a proper scientific field of study, " stated Nobel Prize Laurette Francis Crick. (Crick F 1994)

A scientific investigation of mediumship must address the following issues if mediumship is a natural phenomenon:

1. Consciousness must be independent of brain function and survive bodily death.
2. Information must be able to be stored outside of the human mind/brain.
3. The human mind/brain must be able to interact with this information, accessing and transmitting it meaningfully.
4. Reality must be a coherent, integrated system in which accessing and processing information can occur independently of time and space.
5. One's individual personal sense of "I" or an individual consciousness must be able to interact with discarnate clusters of information, which also have a sense of individual consciousness, or if part of a universal consciousness, must be able to communicate as if a coherent individual entity.
6. Neurobiological structures must facilitate this information transfer and a neurobiological mechanism for translating information possessed by discarnate entities into a form that can be transmitted, accessed, and properly interpreted by the individual's mind/brain.

1.- Death is Just a Body Problem

Strong scientific evidence now suggests that consciousness survives the death of the body. This comes from 1) Near-death research and 2) Anecdotal reports and observational studies, which seemingly can only be explained by an individual consciousness surviving the body's death.

"The conflict between current neuroscientific orthodoxy and the occurrence of NDEs . . is head-on, profound, and inescapable." (Greyson. B, Irreducible Mind 2007 pp 423) Dr. Greyson, Professor Emeritus of Psychiatry at the University of Virginia, states that both prospective and retrospective studies document that the dying

process includes an expanded sense of consciousness and the perception of a timeless, spaceless conscious reality often populated by individual conscious "spirits."(Greyson B., 2007)

Studies documenting that the NDE is the dying experience and not a confabulation after the fact include the American Journal of Heart (Burch G.E. 1968) and, more recently, have been published in The Lancet (van Lommel P. 2001) and American Medical Association Pediatric Journals. (Morse 1985) Michael Sabom published a prospective study documenting that patients' perceptions during their NDEs were accurate compared to control patients' perceptions. (Sabom 1982)

That the dying process involves an expanded sense of awareness beyond the body is clearly documented in an experimental study of the processes of death done by the United States National Warfare Institute. Navy fighter pilots were assessed on their ability to withstand gravitational forces by spinning them in centrifuges. After the pilots slip into a coma and are theoretically at the point of death, they report a return to consciousness at the point of death with an extended awareness outside the physical body. (Whinnery 1990))

BICS has published a comprehensive compilation of the evidence for survival after bodily death (BICS 2023). The evidence is presented in 28 essays from the top researchers worldwide, including Dutch cardiologist Pin von Lommel MD, Jeffrey Mishlove Ph.D., Stephen Braude Ph.D., Jeffrey Long MD, and Leo Ruickbie Ph.D.

2.- "Information is the Only Thing that Exists"

So wrote Professor Paul Davies, an Arizona State theoretical physicist and astrobiologist who was an early pioneer in Information Theory (Davies P 2010)

By the late 20th century, several theoretical physicists began to realize that the quantum substrate of reality was a perfect reservoir for information and its processing. (Gleick J 2011)(Lloyd S 2007)(Vedral V 2010) John Wheeler (Professor of Physics Princeton) proposed that physics be recast as information theory; he postulated that "every it-every particle, every field of force, even the spacetime continuum itself derives its function, its meaning, its very existence entirely from the apparatus elicited answers to yes or no questions, binary choices, bits . . . . . .(indicating) this is a participatory universe." (Wheeler 1990)

3.- The Brain as a Read-Write Head of Information

One model of consciousness and memory is that the brain is a "read-write head" of an information-processing biological organism (a human) interacting with the electromagnetic field that the physicists state represents the substrate of reality. Accordingly, the experimental findings support the hypothesis that the brain produces consciously perceived memory traces in the stimulus-oriented operating mode by writing sequences of information states into the universal electromagnetic reality. (Keppler J 2024 Table 2)(Horner A et al 2017)(Hiibjers W et al. 2011)(Idris Z. 2021)

4.- Top-Down Causation and a Conscious Universe

Inherent in complex systems and information theory is top-down causation, meaning that organizing principles unify scientific understandings of reality. Top-down causation permits mediumship as it states that a universal consciousness organizes and interacts with this physical reality, including individual minds and brains. In contrast, Materialism is a bottom-up causation theory that would not permit mediumship, as consciousness, in that model, exists only as a byproduct of an individual mind or brain.

Robert Lanza, one of the world's most respected scientists, proposed his model of biocentrism, which he described as "We genome-based creatures all share a common biological (spatiotemporal) information-processing ability. I have previously written about how reality is not a hard, cold thing but rather an active process that involves our consciousness. According to biocentrism, space and time are simply the tools our mind uses to weave information together into a coherent experience — they are the language of consciousness." (Lanza R. 2020)

Other scientists who have proposed their own theories of how individual minds interact with a conscious universe include Stu Hammeroff and Nobel Laureate Roger Penrose (Lahey S 2023), Niele Theise MD (Theise, 2023), and Nobel Laureate Frank Wilczek (Wilczek F 2021). Dr. Wilczek stated that his research led him to "study how God works and what God is." (Wilczek F 2021 page xiii)

5.- The Soul is a Cluster Of Information

So says Michael Shermer, writing in Scientific American. "The soul is a pattern of information that represents you—your thoughts, memories, and personality—your self" (Shermer, 2016). Information theory states that information is eternal and embedded in the very structure of reality. If Dr. Shermer is correct, then discrete clusters of information can have a separate sense of consciousness unique to that cluster of information; in religious terms, this would be called "a soul."

In an entangled conscious universe, it is a reasonable scientific speculation to propose that individual clusters of information, or souls, can communicate with each other, whether or not they are associated with a physical body. If the universe is a top-down integrated universe organized as a complex system, then the conscious universe itself or individual components of it could communicate with human mind/brains, which is the essential element of mediumship

6.- The Brain is an Antenna

In 1997, University of San Diego Neuroscientists published that they found a "god module" in the right temporal lobe, demonstrating that "the human brain may be hard-wired to hear the voice of heaven." (Ramachandran V.S. 1998) These neuroscientific findings were integrated with clinical research on near-death experiences (Morse, 2004) and spiritual perceptions (Beauregard, 2008), demonstrating that the perception of communicating with a spiritual universe is a normal human ability linked to specific neurobiological structures.

Miguel Gaona, MD, Ph.D., is arguably the world's expert on this subject. His research covers every aspect of the brain as an antenna, from studies showing that information can be implanted in the brain remotely to studies showing that information can be accessed from the brain also remotely. (Gaona 2015).

Wet, Warm Brains are Capable of Quantum Processes

For the individual mind/brain to interact with consciousnesses outside of the brain, quantum processes must be able to function in the warm, wet environment of the human brain. Biological systems have been shown to function non-locally (meaning at a quantum level), resulting in a new field of quantum biology (Marais, 2021). Birds have been shown to use quantum processes for migration (Levy, 2021), cats for color vision (Marais, 2021), and plants for photosynthesis. (Cao 2020) There is even speculation that Major League baseball players use non-locality in hitting a fastball.

It is a Reasonable Scientific Speculation to Use

the Human Brain to Access Wisdom From a Conscious Universe

As illustrated above, these six criteria for what must be valid for mediumship to be real have adequate scientific support. ISSC does not intend to comment on which current scientific theories are correct. It is enough that it is demonstrated that empirical evidence from mainstream scientists exists, indicating that science is in the middle of a paradigm shift, which will ultimately result in mediumship being understood as a natural human ability. This current project could be conceptualized as a hypothesis-generating study that results in further studies that might advance scientific understandings of consciousness.

VIII.- References

Anderson C. (2000). From molecules to mindfulness. *Consciousness and Emotion* 1 (2), 193-226

Armstrong K (2006). The Great Transformation: The birth of religious traditions. Alfred Knopf

Barna. (2017, May 26). Church attendance trends around the country. Retrieved March 9, 2024, from https://www.barna.com/research/church-attendance-trends-around-country/

Behrendt, R. P. (2013). Conscious experience and episodic memory: Hippocampus at the crossroads. Frontiers in Psychology, 4, 304. https://doi.org/10.3389/fpsyg.2013.00304

Baksa, P. (2011). The zero point field: How thoughts become matter. The Huffington Post. Retrieved March 12, 2024, from https://www.huffpost.com/entry/zero-point-field_b_913831

Bigelow Institute for Consciousness Studies. (2023) *Winning Essays: Proof of Survival of Human Consciousness Beyond Permanent Bodily Death.*

Bierman, D. J., & Radin, D. I. (1997). Anomalous anticipatory response on randomized future conditions. Perceptual and Motor Skills, 84(3), 689-690.

Encyclopedia Britannica. (n.d.). History and society: The Enlightenment. Retrieved March 10, 2024, from https://www.britannica.com/event/Enlightenment-European-history

Brubaker, B. (2021, July 20). How Bell's theorem proved 'spooky action at a distance' is real. Quanta Magazine.

https://www.quantamagazine.org/how-bells-theorem-proved-spooky-action-at-a-distance-is-real-20210720/

Burke, J. (1995). The day the universe changed: How Galileo's telescope changed the truth and other events in history that dramatically altered our understanding of the world. Bay Back Books.

Cao, J. (2020, April 3). Quantum biology revisited. Science Advances, 6(14). https://doi.org/10.1126/sciadv.aaz4888

Carducci, B. (2020). Carl Jung. In Wiley Encyclopedia of Personality and Individual Differences: Models and Theories (Chapter 13). https://doi.org/10.1002/9781119547143.ch13

Cartwright, J. (2024, January 31). The quantum world: A concise guide to the particles that make reality. New Scientist. https://www.msn.com/en-us/news/technology/the-quantum-world-a-concise-guide-to-the-particles-that-make-reality/ar-AA1c8S7J

Chance, B. (1937, May). Sir Clifford Allbutt: Apostle of medical ophthalmology. Archives of Ophthalmology, 17, 612-625. https://jamanetwork.com/journals/jamaophthalmology/article-abstract/612893

Chauffeton Saavedra, I. (2013). God consciousness: The journey of a science-driven psychic medium. Survival of Consciousness LLC.

Chauffeton Saavedra, I. (2016). Therefore, I think - New Edition: A Psychic Medium's Insight into the Emergence of Consciousness in the Universe—survival of Consciousness LLC.

Cottrell, C. (2024, January 3). Personal communications based on her expertise as a trainer of mediums as to the classification of mediums. Retrieved from https://carolcottrell.com/

Crick, F. (1994). The astonishing hypothesis: The scientific search for the soul. Charles Scribner.

CRV-REG Study. (2024, January 31). Sponsored by the International Remote Viewers Association. Retrieved from https://www.crvreg.org/

Davies, P. (2010). Information and the nature of reality. Cambridge University Press.

Eagleman, D. (Writer), & Barden, G. (Director). (2015, October 1). What is reality? [Television series episode]. In J. Kershaw (Executive Producer), The Brain with David Eagleman: PBS series. Blink Films.

Encyclopedia.com. (n.d.). Philosophy and science. Retrieved March 10, 2024, from https://www.encyclopedia.com/religion/encyclopedias-almanacs-transcripts-and-maps/philosophy-and-science

Fahrenheit, D. (1724). Experimenta circa gradum caloris liquorum nonnullorum ebullientium instituta. Philosophical Transactions of the Royal Society. https://royalsocietypublishing.org/doi/10.1098/rstl.1724.0002

Faithful Seeker. (2023). The faith and philosophy of Sir Isaac Newton: Unraveling the spiritual journey of a scientific genius. Retrieved March 12, 2024, from https://hopenomatterwhat.com/the-faith-and-philosophy-of-isaac-newton-unraveling-the-spiritual-journey-of-a-scientific-genius/

Fred Hutchinson Cancer Research Center. (2002, July 2). More than half of the 'best doctors' in Western Washington are from Children's, Fred Hutchinson, Harborview, UW Medical Center, and VA Medical Center. Retrieved April 12, 2024, from https://www.fredhutch.org/en/news/releases/2002/07/best_doctors.html

Garisto, D. (2022, October 6). The universe is not locally real and the Physics Nobel Prize winners proved it. Scientific American. Retrieved from https://www.scientificamerican.com/article/the-universe-is-not-locally-real-and-the-physics-nobel-prize-winners-proved-it/

Gaona, J. (2022). On the other side of the tunnel: A journey to the brink of death to the light beyond. Secret Media Publishers.

Gaona, J. (2015). The limit: A deep investigation into the brain, consciousness, and near-death experiences. Whole Sphere Books. ISBN 8490608814.

Gleick, J. (2011). The information. Pantheon Books.

Greyson, B. (2007). Near-death experiences. In E. Kelly, E. Kelly, A. Crabtree, A. Gauld, M. Grosso, & B. Greyson (Eds.), Irreducible mind: Towards a psychology for the 21st century (pp. 459–347). Rowman & Littlefield Publishers.

Hardwerk, B. (2021, February 22). An evolutionary timeline of Homo sapiens. Smithsonian Magazine. Retrieved from https://www.smithsonianmag.com/science-nature/essential-timeline-understanding-evolution-homo-sapiens-180976807/

Huijbers, W., Pennartz, C. M. A., Cabeza, R., & Daselaar, S. M. (2011). The hippocampus is coupled with the default network during memory retrieval but not during memory encoding. PLoS One, 6(e17463). https://doi.org/10.1371/journal.pone.0017463

Horgan, J. (2011, March 7). Why information can't be the basis of reality. Scientific American. Retrieved from https://www.scientificamerican.com/article/why-information-cant-be-the-basis-of-reality/

Horner, A. J., Bisby, J. A., Bush, D., Lin, W., & Burgess, N. (2015). Evidence for holistic episodic recollection via hippocampal pattern completion. Nature Communications, 6(7462). https://doi.org/10.1038/ncomms8462

Howard, D. A., & Giovanelli, M. (2019). Einstein's philosophy of science. In E. N. Zalta (Ed.), The Stanford Encyclopedia of Philosophy (Fall 2019 edition). Retrieved from https://plato.stanford.edu/archives/fall2019/entries/einstein-philscience/

Irva.org. (2024, January 31). Warcollier Prize 2011. Retrieved from https://www.irva.org/page/2?s=Warcollier+Prize

Jahn R, Dunne BJ (2007 May/June) The Pertinence of the Princeton Engineering Anomalies Research Laboratory to the Pursuit of Global Health. *Explore: The Journal of Science and Healing* Special Edition (3) 3

Kaku, M. (2021). The God equation: A quest for the theory of everything. Doubleday.

Kapraff, J. (2002). Beyond measure: A guided tour through nature, myth, and number. World Scientific Publishing.

Kardec, A. (2006). *The spirits' book* (D. et al. Saiz, Trans.). International Spiritist Council. (Original work published 1857).

Kardec, A. (1876). The mediums' handbook (A. et al..). Pantianos Classics. (Original work published 1861)

Kardek, A. (1987). The gospel according to spiritism. (J. A. Duncan, Trans.). The Headquarters Publishing Co., Ltd. (Original work published 1866).

Keppler, J. (2020, January 10). The common basis of memory and consciousness: Understanding the brain as a write–read head interacting with an omnipresent background field. Frontiers in Psychology. https://doi.org/10.3389/fpsyg.2019.02968

Knox, R., Hambly, N., Hawkens, H., et al. (1998, July). Digital stacking of photographic plates with SuperCOSMOS. Monthly Notices of the Royal Astronomical Society.

Koch, C. (2014, January). Is consciousness universal? Scientific American.

Korzen, M. Z. (2016, November 16). The Semmelweis effect. Ohio State University. Retrieved March 24, 2024, from https://u.osu.edu/korzen.1/2016/11/26/the-semmelweis-reflex-or-semmelweis-effect-is-a-metaphor-for-the-reflex-like-tendency-to-reject-new-evidence-or-new-knowledge-because-it-contradicts-established-norms-beliefs-or-paradigms/

Kuhn, T. (1962). The structure of scientific revolutions. The University of Chicago Press.

Lahey, S. (2023, October 8). Your very own consciousness can interact with the whole universe, scientists believe. Popular Mechanics. Retrieved from http://science/a45574179/architecture-of-consciousness/

Lanza, R. (2020, May 18). The biocentric universe theory: Life creates time, space, and the cosmos itself. Discover Magazine. Retrieved from https://www.discovermagazine.com/the-sciences/the-biocentric-universe-theory-life-creates-time-space-and-the-cosmos-itself

Leibovici, L. (2001). The effects of remote retroactive intercessory prayer on outcomes in patients with bloodstream infections: Randomized controlled trial. British Medical Journal, 323, 1450-1451.

Levy, A. (2021, June 16). How quantum biology could help birds 'see' magnetic fields. Nature. https://doi.org/10.1038/d41586-021-01725-1

Lloyd, S. (2007). Programming the universe. Vintage Books.

Lohrey, A., & Boreham, B. (2020, October 11). The nonlocal universe. Communicative and Integrative Biology. Retrieved from https://www.ncbi.nlm.nih.gov/pmc/articles/PMC7588183/

Matter. (2024). National Geographic. Retrieved March 12, 2024, from https://education.nationalgeographic.org/resource/matter/

McCraty, R., Atkinson, M., & Bradley, R. T. (2004). Electrophysiological evidence of intuition: Part 2. A system-wide process? Journal of Alternative and Complementary Medicine, 10(2), 325-.

Montague, U., & Krippner, S. (1989). Dream studies and telepathy. Parapsychology Foundation New York.

Morse, M. L., Savich, J., & Bleyer, A. (1985). Altered central nervous system pharmacology of methotrexate in childhood leukemia. Journal of Clinical Oncology, 3(1), 19–25.

Morse, M. L., Milstein, J., & Haas, J. (1985). The effect of hydration on experimentally induced cerebral edema. Critical Care Medicine, 13(7), 563-565.

Morse, M. L., & Beem-Williams, L. (2011, December). Benefits of Reiki therapy for a severely neutropenic patient with associated influences on a true random number generator. Journal of Complementary and Alternative Medicine.

Morse, M. L. (1990). Closer to the light: Learning from the near-death experiences of children. Ballantine Books.

Morse, M. L. (1994). Near-death experiences and death-related visions for the clinician. Current Problems in Pediatrics, pp. 24, 55–83.

Morse, M. L. (2013). The positive potential of dissociative states of consciousness. In E. Bragdon (Ed.), Spiritist and mental health practices from Spiritist centers and Spiritist psychiatric hospitals in Brazil (pp. 212–218, 319–320). Singing Dragon Philadelphia.

Morse, M., & Saavedra, I. (2014). Spiritual sight: The manual. Amazon On Demand.

Morse, M. L. (1983). A near-death experience in a 7-year-old child. American Journal of Diseases of Children, pp. 137, 959–961.

Morse, M. L. (2000, December). The right temporal lobe and associated limbic lobe structures as an interface with an interconnected universe. The Network: The Scientific and Medical Network Review, p. 74.

Morse, M. L., Castillo, P., & Venecia, D. (1985). Childhood near-death experiences. American Journal of Diseases of Children, 140, 110-114.

Morse, M. L., & Neppe, V. M. (1991). Near-death experiences. The Lancet, 337, 386.

Musser, G. (2015). Spooky action at a distance. Scientific American Books.

Naifeh, S. W. (1996, May). The best doctors in America: Pacific Northwest region 1996-1997. BI Rankings LLC.

Nelson, K. (2012). The spiritual doorway in the brain: A neurologist's search for the God experience. Plume.

Lahav, N., Sendiña-Nadal, I., Hens, C., et al. (2022). Topological synchronization of chaotic systems. Sci Rep, 12, 2508. Retrieved from https://doi.org/10.1038/s41598-022-06262-z

Pappas, S. (2022, September 27). How does the brain store memories? Live Science. Retrieved March 12, 2024, from https://www.livescience.com/how-the-brain-stores-memories

Parr, A. J. (2014). Living in the now in easy steps: Understanding Eckhart Tolle, Dalai Lama, Krishnamurti, and more. Grapevine Books.

Parr, A. J. (2023). Stairway to Heaven: 25 near-death experiences about encounters with God, Jesus, and Paradise (Journalistic research on real cases). Grapevine Books.

Parr, A. J. (2020). The secret teachings of Jesus: And the mystery of the first Christians. Grapevine Books.

Penfield, W. (1955). The role of the temporal cortex in certain psychical phenomena. Journal of Mental Science, 101(3), 451–465.

Pitkaanen M. (2001 Quantum criticality and $1/f$ noise *Fluctuation and Noise Letters* • http://www.maths.ex.ac.uk/~mwatkins/zeta/qcand1fnoise.pdf

Powell, D. H. (2009). The ESP enigma: The scientific case for psychic phenomena. Walker Publishing.

Puthoff, H. E. (1990). Source of electromagnetic zero-point energy. Physical Review A, 40, 4857.

Psyleron.com. (2024, January 31). Psyleron: Consciousness technologies. Retrieved from https://www.psyleron.com/

Spiritism.org. (2024, January 24). What is Spiritism? Retrieved from https://spiritism.org/

Radin, D. (2008). Nonlocal observations as a source of intuitive knowledge. Explore, 4(25), 25–35. © Elsevier Inc. 2008.

Radin, D. (1997). The conscious universe: The scientific proof of psychic phenomena. HarperEdge.

Radin D, Nelson R. (1989). Evidence for Consciousness Related Anomalies in Random Physical Systems. *Foundations of Physics* (19) 12

Ramachandran, V. S., & Blakeslee, S. (1998). Phantoms in the brain. Morrow.

Rocke, A. (2010). Image and reality: Kekule, Kopp, and the scientific imagination. University of Chicago Press.

Sabom, M. B. (1982). Recollections of death: A medical investigation. Harper & Row.

Saver, J., & Rabin, J. (1997). The neural substrates of religious experience. Journal of Neuropsychiatry,

9(4), 498-510.

Schmidt H: (1969) Quantum Processes Predicted? *New Scientist* 33 pp 300-306

Shermer, M. (2016, February 1). Can our minds live forever? Scientific American. Retrieved from https://scientificamerican.com/article/can-our-minds-live-forever/

Smith, George. (2008, Winter). Newton's Philosophiæ Naturalis Principia Mathematica. The Stanford Encyclopedia of Philosophy. Edward N. Zalta (ed.). Retrieved from https://plato.stanford.edu/archives/win2008/entries/newton-principia/

Spiritist Medical Association: International. (2024). Retrieved March 24, 2024, from https://sma-international.org/about/

Stevenson, I. (1980). Twenty cases suggestive of reincarnation: Second edition, revised and enlarged. University of Virginia Press.

Targ, R., & Puthoff, H. (1975). Information transfer under conditions of sensory shielding. Nature, 251, 602-607.

Targ, R., & Puthoff, H. (1980). Information transmission in remote viewing experiments. Nature, 284, 191.

Tegmark, M. (2014). Our mathematical universe: My quest for the ultimate nature of reality. Random House.

The Database for Brain Effectiveness & Memory. (n.d.). Retrieved from https://dbem.org/

The Encyclopedia of Quantum Physics: Quantum Physics Lady. (2019, August 16). Local realism. Retrieved from https://quantumphysicslady.org/glossary/local-realism/

Theise, N. (2023). Notes on complexity: A scientific theory of connection, consciousness, and being. Spiegel and Grau.

Thompkins, M. (2019, May 30). When mystics and mediums convinced scientists the paranormal was normal. Literary Hub. Retrieved from https://lithub.com/when-mystics-and-mediums-convinced-scientists-the-paranormal-was-normal/

Travis, T. (2006, August 31). A forgotten anniversary? Education in Chemistry. Retrieved from https://edu.rsc.org/feature/a-forgotten-anniversary/2020083.article

Tucker, J. (2007). Children who claim to remember previous lives: Past, present, and future research. Journal of Scientific Exploration, 21(3), 543–552.

Vedral, V. (2010). Decoding reality. Oxford University Press.

Whinnery, J. E. (1990). Acceleration-induced loss of consciousness. Archives of Neurology, pp. 47, 764–766.

Zhang, K., & Wang, J. (2024). Quasiprobability fluctuation theorem behind the spread of quantum information. Commun Phys, pp. 7, 91. Retrieved from https://doi.org/10.1038/s42005-024-01583-z

Appendix

Additional BICS Questions 1

Melvin L. Morse, MD

SQ 1|

On Help Received in the Last 100 Years

Give specific examples from the last 100 years of how the Other Side has fostered, helped, or accelerated human spiritual evolution.

Examples include inspiring scientific inventions (radio, telephone, cell phone, the internet), medical advancements (vaccines, ocular surgery, blood types and transplants), social movements like the Civil Rights, key figures such as Martin Luther King Jr., Thomas Alba Edison, Albert Einstein, and Nicolas Tesla are examples, as well as tragic events like 9/11, the World Wars, and the Oklahoma bombings.

Several entities indicated they were responsible for all man's spiritual progress. One entity made the difficult-to-understand comment that anything good is, by definition, from the spiritual world and that there is no separation between the worlds.

SEE BICS QUESTION 3 FOR A COMPLETE RESPONSE.

Kardec Quote:

459. Do spirits have any influence on our thoughts and actions?

"Their influence on you in this regard is greater than you suppose, for very frequently it is they who guide you." (Kardec, 2006, p. 296).

SQ 2

On Self-Extinction and Remedies

Without some shift in planet-wide spirituality to match technological growth, humans are at risk of self-inflicted extinction. If you agree with this statement, please give specific remedies.

The medium's statements are presented in the final section of the answers to Question 1. (Page 42). The remedies specifically mentioned, implied, or alluded to by TOS are presented below.

Remedy 1: Believing in God again

"If we started to believe in God again, God being the maker of all beings, then together (with God), we can make things better. We should be calm and hope for the best. God is the Spirit of energy; you have to be positive-minded to communicate with God; prayer is the connection"

Remedy 2: Connecting with the Spirit World

Humanity is in danger of extinction. The remedy is to find the connection with the spirit world again. Humanity has failed its first test. (That being the Axial Age and the development of the seven major religions) However, there will be more tests and chances for spiritual progress. Humans have an innate desire to connect with the Spirit because that is a source of all power, a source of life. Humans can stop going in a myriad of directions, chasing temporal things, and allow themselves to connect with the one with Spirit. That is what it requires for the world to become, as you say, a good place.

Religion is one way people seek to connect. Humans have many ways of connecting. Some sit by a stream, close their eyes, and feel the Spirit. Some look in the faces of their newborn children and see the Spirit, some climb mountains.

The Spirit is everywhere; it is available to all who ask to be open to being a part of the solution to help.

Remedy 3: Love and spiritual practice

It is all about love. Love your brother, love your sister. We are all one family. We are all from one energy, and it will be a massive conflict trying to get us to get back together, and it will take a lot of time and healing. You are here to learn to love each other. Love will conquer this soon. Meditation, compassion, and love will help. But it can only start with the individual and spread from there. Be humble, realize that nature is bigger than Mankind, and change their relationship with the Earth to be humbler and more spiritual."

Remedy 4: Listening to the Spirit World

You need to learn the importance of listening and not just hearing. It is an understanding when we show you things.

SQ 3

This question concerns a future event shaping humanity's course for decades. At the Spirit World's request, the answer is sealed at this time. Specifically, in our interactions with the spirit of Allan Kardec, he stated that he knew the answer, and we are not to know it at this time. The medium commented that he then "laughed in my face."

SQ 4

On the Other Side's Collective Help

Is spiritual help from the other side focused only on individuals, or can the other side help or influence groups, communities, or countries? If the latter, can you provide specific examples?

Individual actions and spiritual growth contribute to the collective consciousness and the overall evolution of humanity. However, the mediums' responses to all the questions clearly show that they act primarily on the individual. This can come in the form of inspiration, inventions, gentle nudges, and intuitions.

One example given was that the spirit world influenced children to play in a specific location so that they would witness a motorcycle accident and call for help. Another example is that they influenced someone to take a job in another city to promote spiritual progress.

They acknowledge that it is up to the individual to decide if a thought is spiritually inspired or born of their fears and prejudices.

SEE BICS QUESTION # 2

Kardec Quote:

"Spirits constantly act upon the mental world and even upon the physical world. They act upon matter and thought. They comprise one of the powers of nature. They are the actual cause behind many phenomena that have been unexplainable or poorly explained until now, and which have not found a rational solution except in Spiritism." (Kardec, 2006, p. 43)

SQ 5

On the Other Side's Shifting Effort

There are periodic increases in intensity during some epochs when the "other side" makes a stronger effort to deepen or increase human spiritual evolution. If you disagree with this statement, give specific reasons. If you agree with this statement, give specific reasons.

Human progress is cyclical, marked by periods of awakening, introspection, and even setbacks. Throughout history, there have been periods of spiritual awakening and closure. This suggests that humanity goes through spiritual openness and closure phases, each playing a role in the larger journey.

SEE BICS QUESTION 1

Kardec Quote:

783. Does the perfecting of humankind always follow a slow

Progressive march?

"There is the regular slow progress that results from the force of things. However, when a culture does not advance quickly enough, then from time to time, God causes a physical or moral jolt that transforms it." (Kardec, 2006, p. 429-430).

SQ 6

On Effects of Death by War

What effect has the significant increase in human deaths by war, during the 19th and 20th centuries, had on the dynamics of spirit transition to the Other Side? For example, with thousands of soldiers simultaneously entering the afterlife from battle on a given day during war, have individual soldiers been met by their deceased relatives in an orderly manner or has chaos ensued? Please give us as many details as possible in your answers.

Tragedies often spark spiritual progress, bringing people together, as in the World Wars, 9/11, Oklahoma City bombings, and Jonestown. These were created by the I AM to advance human progress and help us spiritually.

Death plays a role in spiritual evolution. After humans die, they become closer to The I AM and can communicate with him, improving communication with the living. No one really dies. Death and life are like a great migration.

As to the specific question of the disruption of the processes of death by a mass influx seen in wars, the entities were clear that we do not understand what happens after death, and they cannot explain it to us, but the short answer is "no."

One medium, when presented with this question while in a trance, spoke in the voice of The Trinity: "I need more soldiers, more angels; that's why so many are dying.

Kardec Quotes:

744. What has been the goal of Providence in making war necessary?

"Freedom and progress."

– If war is meant to bring freedom, why is it that it has usually had subjugation as its objective and result?

"Temporary subjugation enables cultures to evolve more quickly."

743. Will war someday disappear from the earth?

"Yes, when men and women understand justice and practice God's law. Then all nations will live as brothers and sisters."

SQ 7

On 19th Century Golden Age

The "golden age" of scientific engagement with spiritualism and in particular, with mediumship, in the late 19th century comprised luminaries such as Sir William Crookes, Sir Oliver Lodge, Nobel Prize winner Charles Richet all engaging very proactively in testing mediums and in experimentally interrogating those who claimed to communicate with the Other

Side. Can the Other Side suggest steps to regain this momentum of scientific engagement with mediums in 2023? Alternatively, does the Other Side view it as undesirable or unnecessary to regain this momentum? Please be detailed and specific.**

Contrary to the late 19th century, we have been in a dark age of spiritual progress, but we are now emerging and will move forward. People are actively trying to contact the spiritual world. New lines of communication with The Other Side will appear. Earthbound spirits will play a positive role. New technology will help us connect to God, help us be centered, and connect Him and Himself.

Several mediums indicated that BICS and its project should become part of a new scientific engagement with mediumship. It is clear that TOS inspired this Challenge Grant, inspired the 4 Questions, and wants to reengage with scientists similar to the "golden age" of scientific investigation of mediumship seen in the later 19th century.

SEE BICS QUESTION 2 & 3.

SQ 8

On others impeding human progress

Are you (spirits on the other side) aware of any spirits, non-human entities or other intelligences that impede, sabotage, or distort the progress of human spiritual evolution? Please give detailed answers.

Yes, some spirits and entities with no interest in letting humans evolve feed off of chaos, negative energies, and turmoil; they can sometimes cause humans to have angry, hateful thoughts so that they can impede us in this limited manner. It is part of how the world is set up. All we hope is that there will be more openness to receiving and being a part of making the human experience more powerful for the journey of love.

It is clear that bad or evil spirits cannot directly affect humanity. They work by clouding people's minds and fostering chaos and hatred. The role of lies and a "veil of lies" are repeatedly mentioned as primary ways that bad spirits affect humans. Humans have free will and choices and always have direct access to spiritual guidance through prayer, paying attention to their inner voices, and listening to the numerous spirit guides and angels that are a regular part of their lives. It is up to the individual to do this.

Medium 0115's entity, "the voices who speak as one," was most eloquent.

We go back to what we said in the beginning, which is that there is good and bad in every human being. It is how that human chooses to connect with spirit or not connect with one that will help determine whether they go forth in light or in darkness. And many are afraid. They don't know. They can't allow themselves to open themselves to spirit. What you call bad is not spirit; it is lack of spirit. The dark side is the lack of spirit.

Monitor :

Well, what can we do about it? What should humans do?

Medium 0115 Trance Voice:

Humans have an innate desire to connect with spirit because that is a source of all power, a source of life.

Medium 0115 Trance Voice:

Humans can stop going in a myriad of directions, chasing temporal things, and allow themselves to connect with the one with spirit. That is what it requires for The World

To become, as you say, a good place.

Monitor:

So, I mean, does this happen through religion, or is it just on the individual level? Or how can we foster this connection?

Medium 0115 Trance Voice:

It happens both ways. Religion is one way people seek to connect. Humans have many ways of connecting. Some sit by a stream, close their eyes, and feel the spirit. Some look in the faces of their newborn children and see the spirit. Some climb mountains.

The spirit is everywhere and is available to all who ask to be open to being a part of the whole.

The problem is more complex in that various entities emphasize that humans must look within to find wisdom. Yet Medium 0110 states that humans often cannot tell the difference between input from bad spirits and true connectedness with spirit.

Part of the human spiritual journey is learning to distinguish between the lies, hatred, anger, and chaos that bad spirits foster and the more positive thoughts encouraged by spirit guides and angels.

SEE BICS QUESTION 4.

Kardec QuoteS:

"Interaction between spirits and humans is constant. Good spirits encourage us to follow the path of the good. They support us in the trials of life and help us to bear them with courage and resignation. On the other hand, evil spirits encourage us to take the path of evil. It is a pleasure for them when they see us succumb and fall to their level. (Kardec, 2006, p. 43)

99. Are all spirits of the third order altogether evil?

"No, some do neither good nor evil; others, however, take pleasure in evil and are pleased when they find an opportunity for it.

Still others are frivolous or foolish spirits, more mischievous than wicked. These take more pleasure in spite than evil, and they also take pleasure in amusing themselves by vexing people and causing them petty annoyances." (Kardec, 2006, p. 124)

Additional BICS Questions 2

AQ 1

On the gap between tech and spiritual evolution

How does the other side view the gap between human technical and spiritual evolution in the past 170 years? Does the other side view the gap as a problem for humanity? Please give specific details in your answer.

The spirit world anticipated this question. All the positive examples mentioned previously are examples of humans trying to find God's law or Laws of Nature.

Originally, scientists wanted to know more about God's laws and saw their scientific discoveries as spiritual events. Now, they often seek power and glory and do not integrate their scientific discoveries with spiritual understandings, resulting in horrific weapons of self-extinction.

AQ 2

On spiritual help during the last 170 years

Give specific examples from the last 170 years of how the other side has fostered, helped, or accelerated human spiritual progress.

Same answer as supplementary question 1 and question 3

AQ 3

On sabotaging spirits

Are you aware of any examples of spirits from the other side sabotaging,

interfering with, or impeding human spiritual progress? Please give specific examples.

Same answer as Supplementary Question 8 and BICS Question 4

Essentially, this answer is yes, there are spirits who interfere with, impede, and sabotage human progress, but the blame is directly placed on humans who don't listen and succumb to hatred, anger, envy, jealousy, and embrace lies, which are directly responsible for the significant lack of progress of the human spiritual journey.

AQ 4

On forbidden information

Is there information that is available to some spirits on the other side that is embargoed or forbidden to be transmitted to living people (while they are still alive)? a. If so, why? b. Who makes the rules?

When Alan Kardec's spirit was asked this question, he responded, "Hidden, but not forbidden." Several mediums mentioned a "key" that will bring greater understanding. There was little clarity on the nature of this key. It was described as "hidden," but at other times, it was indicated that many people held pieces of the key. Whatever this "key" is, it was indicated that it is not for humans at this time as they lack the moral and ethical wisdom necessary to understand it.

Kardec Quote:

18. Will they ever be able to grasp the mystery of things now hidden from them?

"The veil is lifted as they become more and more purified, but in order to understand certain things they need faculties they do not yet have." (Kardec, 2006, p. 87).

AQ 5

On beneficial information

Is there scientific, engineering, technical or new spiritual information that could benefit humanity on the other side that is available and can be accessed by living humans now (in 2023-2024)?

a. If yes, can you give examples?

No specific answers were given that had any practical implications or even details that could be independently evaluated. However, in answer to Additional Question 6, one medium stated: "Now he is showing me a machine that will allow us to contact nonhuman intelligence. He says that pieces of it are already available but it is not complete.

b. If yes, how can humans best access this information from the other side?

We received no specific answers to this, only generalities and vague answers. The answer seemed to be "yes," but there were no specifics on accessing this information.

When the spirit of Allan Kardec was asked this question, he first indicated that humans are an "endangered species." The medium was then shown an image of a cloth or veil covering the earth. The medium stated: It feels like a great discovery, from another time, another planet. But it spreads understanding, knowledge and consciousness.

As an important aside, while we were interviewing the Charleston mediums on this question, one of their friends was present as she assisted in transportation. She stated that she had had a vision the night before in which she was to present information to the ISSC team as they would know for whom the vision was meant. This vision involved aerospace technology that would be discovered soon. The vision was faithfully transmitted to the BICS staff.

AQ 6

On reincarnation

Do all humans reincarnate on earth or do some spirits choose never to incarnate?

a. What is the average length of time between incarnations?

b. Do humans incarnate on other planets?

c. Do non-humans incarnate on earth as humans?

Please give as much detail as possible in the answers to the above questions

Regarding this question, the spirit of Alan Kardec responded:

Can humans reincarnate as non-humans?

Kardec: No.

Do humans reincarnate at all?

Kardec: Yes.

How long does it take between incarnations?

The entity just snapped its fingers, then laughed and said "A millennium".

Are aliens the same as humans?

The Medium: He doesn't like the term aliens. He says they are nonhuman intelligences. They share DNA with humans, but humans only reincarnate as humans, and they only reincarnate as nonhumans.

Several of the mediums answered this question. No more information was gleaned, and no details were given.

AQ 7

On alien and discarnate human relationship

Is there a relationship between extraterrestrials and discarnate humans in the Afterlife? Is there communication between extraterrestrials and humans on the other side? Please give as much detail as possible in your answer.

Not answered in any meaningful way by several mediums who attempted this question.

AQ 8

On individual and collective spiritual help

Is spiritual help from the other side focused only on individuals, or can the other side help or influence groups, communities, or countries?

If the latter, can you provide examples?

Same as supplementary question 4. This is extensively discussed in BICS questions 2 and 3. In brief, their role is primarily with the individual. One example was given of school shootings. The spirit world could not affect the shooters, but often interventions with the victims to show them places to hide, how to pretend to be dead, and other instructions which might not have been perceived as coming from a spiritual source.

AQ 9

On evidential validation

Can you make contact, with the spirits of Reverend Stainton Moses, the entity named Imperator (who communicated with Stainton Moses and Leonora Piper) or the spirit of Allen Kardec (Hippolyte Léon Denizard Rivail)?

Yes. The spirit of Allan Kardec was successfully contacted by two different mediums.

If yes,

a. Can you provide evidential validation that you are in contact with the particular spirit or entity?

The mediums were given the number 598237821. Since the numbers corresponded to questions up until this point, the mediums were not prepared or front-loaded to indicate that now they were to contact a specific discarnate entity.

Medium 0001. She was not told she would be contacting an entity. She was only told that ICCS had a special target for her to work. She had previously worked with other targets for us, including helping to find a lost dog, attempting to heal a woman with severe atrial fibrillation, and successfully identifying a missing person as having committed suicide and the location of his body. So, there was no hint that we now had a very different question for her.

After receiving the target number, she describe a dead person who looked like Allan Kardc She then drew a picture of a steam trunk from the 1800s and stated it was a trunk of knowledge. Spiritists refer to Kardec's five books as the Trunk of Knowledge. This is not found in English translations of his work.

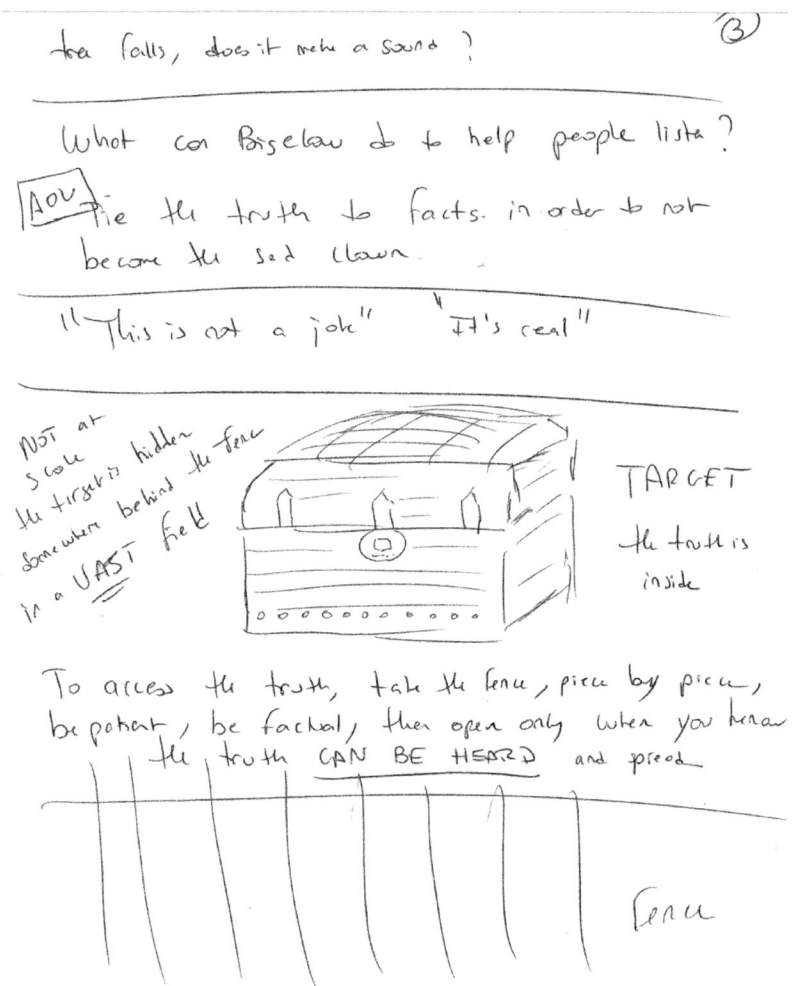

Medium 0114, upon being given the same number stated that the target was a "man, not alive." She smelled decay. She then encountered a barrier and was encouraged to go through it. She called out to see if anyone was present. She was met with a sense of eagerness, excitement, and energy. She could see a face that was full and heavy at the bottom, with sideburns and some hair at the bottom. At the top of the head was a vision of fireworks.

b. Tell us the result of your contact

Additional Questions Posed to Allan Kardec

Medium 1014: She asked it for a name and she heard several names that she did not recognize as names, and then a sense of "one who walks beside". She stated that the I AM was also present, but not speaking.

She said that the person was watching our project with interest.

BICS Question 1: Mankind's progress in the past 166 years: Medium: I got the word "backwards" in a very hard push. Backwards.

Monitor: What can we do about it?

Kardec (through the medium): Stop fighting. There is an internal struggle. Within the human world, not the spiritual world.

BICS Supplemental Question 4 Kardec (through the medium): It is a personal one on one, a walk beside.

Monitor: Is he walking beside any of us now?

The Medium: You, He says you. That was clear.

Monitor: Can you validate for us that you are Allan Kardec?

The Medium: I heard the word "totem" and he is showing me a totem pole. I don't know what it means. He says "you know" and "Odie". I don't know what that is. He says he is beside you all the time."

(The monitor's daughter is called Ody as an extremely private nickname, and she is unaware anyone else knows it. Furthermore, she was not part of this project. She lives thousands of miles from the medium. The message is private and has a specific meaning for the monitor. It is included as it unequivocally validates that the medium contacted the spirit of Allan Kardec.

BICS Supplemental Question 2: Is mankind at the point of extinction because of our technological growth or lack of spiritual growth or both?

Kardec: It is too late.

The Medium: I just heard "devastation".

BICS Supplemental Question 3: Presented as the number 721110524

The Medium: He says he will not say. He just laughed, I mean he just laughed in my face. Other mediums indicated that the answer is sealed at this time.

Additional BICS question 2: Can you give us examples of how the other side has helped us?

The Medium: He is showing me sidewalks. Now he is showing me a medical procedure on the eye.

Now he is showing me bloody body parts, something for mankind's good, like transplant technology.

Something that is for mankind's good.

It kind of scared me so he stopped showing it to me, I mean it was like it was coming at my eye.

Supplemental question 7 The "golden age" of scientific engagement with spiritualism and in particular, with mediumship, in the late 19th century comprised luminaries such as Sir William Crookes, Sir Oliver Lodge, Nobel Prize winner Charles Richet all engaging very proactively in testing mediums and in experimentally interrogating those who claimed to communicate with the Other Side. Can the Other Side suggest steps to regain this momentum of scientific engagement with mediums in 2023? Alternatively does the Other Side view it as undesirable or unnecessary to regain this momentum? Please be detailed and specific.

Kardec: It is happening. It is coming. You (Both ISSC and BICS) are part of it. We want it to happen. It must happen.

Additional Question 3: Are you aware of any examples of spirits from the other side sabotaging, interfering with, or impeding human spiritual progress? Please give specific examples.

The Medium: He is talking to me. A lot. What I got out of it is that it's people. Not spirits. There is human interference, I'm not certain if it is personal or collective.

Supplemental Question 5: There are periodic increases in intensity during some epochs when the "other side" makes a stronger effort to deepen or increase human spiritual evolution. If you disagree with this statement, give specific reasons. if you agree with this statement, give specific reasons.

The Medium: He is showing me a spiral. It seems to be going forward and backwards, but he is showing me an arrow on it which shows it is constantly moving upwards.

Supplemental Question 6 The Medium: Has chaos ensured? I heard "no" but also I heard screams so I don't know how to interpret that. "That was really interesting. I saw a single person on the spiral traveling the spiral and then I got a wave of energy. I can see that there's one person following the spiral and then a wave of energy behind coming this way. The thing is traveling that way and the energy's traveling this way. I don't know how to interpret that."

Supplemental Question 2. First of all, is there a gap between our spirituality and our technological advancement?

Monitor: Is our technology outstripped our spirituality? Are we are risk of extinction because we can't control our technology?

The Medium: I got a clear picture of the technology of a catapult, one of those old-time things that they pull back and they let it go and it just flings forward. Yeah, there's that. Yeah, there's restlessness in the between restlessness. Yeah. I don't even know how to, I see kind of rocks or something moving almost like an earthquake, but I don't feel the ground moving.

He is showing me the catapult to try to highlight his point.

The Monitor: Okay, so me just say something and then see if this entity agrees or disagrees. The catapult (Or Trebuchet) at its time was a fearsome weapon of war that was thought to actually was considered immoral. Is that an example of the nuclear bomb today or the other weapons of war that our technology Is that similar to the catapult as it was in its time?

Kardec: Yes, stop. Stop. Stop using them, you will all be destroyed.

The Medium: He is showing me that technology and spirituality are related, they are together, there is an undulation of both of them, moving together. (The medium moves her hands together as if waving them together.)

Kardec also answered questions on reincarnation, technology and spirituality which have already been presented above.

BICS Supplementary Question 2 (again): No he says its too late. He is sad, dejected. It seems like he is begging for us to help, to listen to him.

Monitor: What else does he have to tell us?

The Medium: He is talking about your project. He wants you to affirm that it is really him. (The medium doesn't know the name of the entity she has contacted) He says that the validation is with you, he is pointing right at the computer, and he is saying "Odie" again.

Monitor's note: Kardec seems to be saying that the BICS project is extremely important in preventing mankind's self-extinction and that he gave such a specific answer concerning the monitor's daughter because he wanted to provide clear and convincing validation that we have contacted him.

The medium is now coming out of trance, retracing the signal line that was created when she entered into trance. She states that something new has been added to the signal line of the target, of the entity, something new has been created as a result of our interaction with Allan Kardec but she is not clear what it is.

Limitations of the BICS Study

John B. Alexander, Ph.D.

"Has the Spirit World failed to enhance human spirituality on Earth since 1857 as evidenced by the dramatic rise in wars, violence and uncontrolled technology at the expense of human spirituality?"

BICS Challenge

While the independent responses to the BICS questions are interesting, it is my opinion that the central concept (Has the Spirit World Failed Humanity?) was flawed from its inception. That, I'll explain shortly. However, that does not mean the results of the exercise are not worth noting.

In my opinion, the central concept has had a series of limitations from the beginning. The questions make several assumptions that cannot be overlooked. Unfortunately, the BICS generated questions were both limiting and leading in their construction.

As can be seen in the methodology, some, but not all, of the negative impacts were mitigated by the remote viewing protocols employed in this study. By substituting randomly assigned numbers for the actual questions, the study minimized the overtly leading aspects of those questions. Still, at a consciousness level, there was a mental connection between the written words and the remote viewing designation.

The promulgating document by BICS appears to point to a serious flaw in the project. Specifically, it states, "Since Allan Kardec optimistically predicted in 1857 an end to wars and conflict in the conclusion of his book *The Spirit's Book,* even a cursory examination of history in the past 166 years shows that the exact opposite of an end to conflicts, war, and seriously negative human behavior has happened." While the above statement is factually correct, it fails to cover the rationale for using it in a guiding document for this research project.

Allan Kardec, a pseudonym for Hippolyte Léon Denizard Rivail, was a renowned 19th-century educator and is considered by many people to be the progenitor of Spiritism. His works are better known in other parts of the world and provided guidance for thousands to follow. It appears that Kardec, like most mediums, no matter how proficient, while seemingly better than his peers, did not have access to all information and was not omniscient. As is known, there have been two World Wars, and many other conflicts since 1856. Therefore, using Kardec as a touchstone is a seriously limiting factor in this exploration. Notably, a spirit self-identifying as Allen Kardec was reported by some of the ISSC mediums in this study and has interacted with other mediums as well.

Unsubstantiated assumptions

In my opinion, the questions posited by BICS have a strong ethnocentric bias. Employing unsubstantiated assumptions regarding the continuity of consciousness beyond bodily death, they appear to ignore the fundamental tenets of major religious belief systems, while leaning heavily in early Judeo-Christian concepts of reincarnation. Many theologians believe reincarnation was dropped from Christianity following the Council at Nicaea in 553 BCE. It is my view, the BICS questions were generated based on Western concepts of religion and the possibility of life after death. With some anecdotal support, they fail to consider the voluminous other NDE reports that are contraindicated by their premise.

To fully respond to the many problems elicited by the BICS questions would take many volumes. For the purpose of this analysis, I will cover some of the most flagrant ones.

Implicit in the BICS questions was the existence of some form of tension between entities in the Spirit World and those of us living in the consensus reality, also known as the "Real World." Note, while it is often reported that near-death experiences are "more real than real" as we know our current reality. For simplicity, I will use the *Real World* throughout the remainder of this analysis. There appears to be a presupposition that *fault* could/must lie on either side of the equation.

BICS Questions Ignored NDE Research

Based on what is known from the many volumes of NDE literature, the issue of culpability for events between Spirit World and Real World (as inhabited by living humans) has never been called into question. Quite the contrary, the vast majority of the NDE literature points to an acceptance of the Earthly situation.

While admittedly imperfect (from a human perspective), the general concept reported from NDEs is that this Earthly lifetime provides for learning experiences. Eternal in nature, those experiences in life are based on the progression of each individual soul. Therefore, the complexities of those interactions are far, far beyond human comprehension,

There is no question that our current sociological, ecological, and physiological status in the physical world (*Real World*) is problematic at best. Given the existence of weapons of mass destruction and the human propensity for violence, it is quite possible we are under an existential threat should a global, or even regional, nuclear confrontation take place.

Speaking in an interview on *Foreign Policy*, Filippo Grandi, High Commissioner of the UN Refugee Agency, stated, "Because of a broken international system," adding, "This is a world that has become unable to make peace." Yes, many bad situations have happened and are continuing to occur. We acknowledge there is a gradient of bad situations that range from personal to global. Consider the existence of disease, accidents, and crime, to famine and wars (large and small). But they are mostly human-generated events.

However, to attribute responsibility for human failings and postmortem activities to the Spirit World is a dramatic stretch. Yet, that is what BICS set out to do.

Implicit in the questions is an unsubstantiated assumption that the Spirit World has some explicit responsibility for events in the Real World. Specifically, they suggest that the Spirit World has responsibility (wholly or partially) for the development of spirituality in the Real World.

Without evidence, the questions also state that some failure has occurred in the development of human spirituality. That runs counter to the many claims by other mediums that things are perfect, not from a human perspective, albeit from a spiritual one.

Direct correlations between Earthly historical events and the information they provided were observed in the responses from some of the mediums. These include descriptions of the origins and purpose of major violent conflicts, catastrophic geological and environmental changes, and major ideological shifts in human perceptions (such as what the purpose of living is).

NDEs & The Relativity of Time

In my opinion, another critical flaw in the generated question was the imposition of time based on human perceptions of its passage. One of the most reported aspects of NDEs is that our (living human) notion of time is completely wrong. Rather, many NDEs indicate that while in that state of consciousness (during their NDE) time, as we know it, does not exist. Often, they reported being exposed to situations and gathering of knowledge that would require an extensive period of "Earth time" to acquire. Yet, the actual duration of the physical NDE was seconds to a few minutes. Some individuals have been afforded accurate foreknowledge of events that will take place years hence. Consider that during her NDE, Dr. Mary Neal was informed that her son would die at a specific age years before the tragic event came to pass. Our traditional belief in linear time passage would not allow for that. It is the human concept of time that concurrently is both wrong yet useful in our Earthly state of existence.

The assumption stated in the BICS tasking explicitly addressed that from 1857 to the present was the duration to be examined by the mediums. If we believe the multitude of NDE reports, and I do, that time designation, as experienced in the Real World, is probably meaningless (or at least beyond human comprehension). It assumes that linear time spent on Earth in human form directly parallels some concept of time as experienced in a Spirit World.

Limitations of The BICS Questions

In addition, several mediums report interactions with spiritual entities that indicate they are reportedly comprised of multiple souls who now act collectively. An excellent example of that is the entity called Sanaya which interacts with the high-profile medium, Suzanne Giesemann. Then there is a fundamental question regarding continuation of consciousness. That is, whether it is personality that survives physical death, or whether there is some form of consciousness merging into an amorphous collective body?

There are also limitations on locations and geography. A question that arises from reincarnation is whether or not Earth is the only destination for human souls. There are numerous reports that souls can migrate and that there exist other life-supporting planets in other galaxies and universes. Additionally, there is substantial information concerning multidimensional possibilities. There are also reports of humans reincarnating in the forms of other species. If so much complexity already is known or hypothesized, why should we assume that the Earth since 1857 is of special concern to those in the Spirit World? Unfortunately, all of those possibilities, and more, are eliminated or truncated by the BICS questions.

In some ways the BICS questions are anachronistic, and reminiscent of a pre-Copernicus, geocentric universe, or even a pre-Galilean heliocentric conception of reality. That, rather than a multidimensional construction, or the known ever-expanding multi-galaxy, multi- universe, one that is revealed astronomically via the Hubble and Webb telescopes. While it may be interesting for mortals to contemplate their personal meaning and scope on Earth's corporeal plane, the vastness and complexities of physical and spiritual existence pale in comparison and cannot/should not be intellectually constrained by the thoughts/whims of Earth-bound humans who seemingly transit this physical reality but for an astronomical instant.

Currently, many countries in the world are gravitating towards nationalism. In America, that is a conservative focal point. For many people, the notion of "globalism" is to be eschewed. Based on the study of the nature of consciousness, it is my view, *"that if you are thinking globally, you are thinking too small."* **Consciousness is limitless and eternal.**

The Brain as an Antenna

José Miguel Gaona, MD

For many; the brain is a simple organ that centralizes all sensations passively and executes cognitive and volitional functions. However, according to my research, it is an organ that acts as an antenna, although it is also very receptive to all types of surrounding stimuli, whether sound, visual through light, or any other of the five senses. In sum, our brains receive and react to physical stimuli coming from our environment, but they also "leave a mark" on that same environment that could be the matrix, as if it were a universal library, a consciousness to which we would all have access. It is nothing less than an antenna, which receives and casts information to the universe at large.

These results are markedly consistent with previous research on important or sacred sites, which have shown significant sonic resonance features within this precise range of frequencies. An additional consideration is applied to the potential effects of 110 Hz physical stimuli on biological systems in the context of neurotheology and the associated biophysical analyses in order to demonstrate the potential importance of 110 Hz signals on religious experience and subjective states of consciousness.[1]

---

1. Archaeoacoustic Investigation of a Prehistoric Cave Site: Frequency-Dependent Sound Amplification and Potential Relevance for Neurotheology. NeuroQuantology | December 2014 | Volume 12 | Issue 4

As has been demonstrated experimentally, the living brain responds to pulsatile electromagnetic fields. The development of living systems from single-cell to multicellular organisms occurred within the geomagnetic field. As Dubrov et al.[2] succinctly summarized, many correlational studies indicate that all organisms respond to some component of geomagnetic activity.

Rajaram et al.[3] and Michon et al.[4] demonstrated that the magnitude of the correlation between spontaneous seizures in epileptic rats and geomagnetic activity during the same intervals was experimentally reproducible when the rats were exposed to a simulated "magnetic storm" pattern generated within the laboratory, a clear demonstration of physical influence on brain activity.

In other words, the brain acts as if it were a true antenna. Some of its energies, through the Faraday Effect, are transformed into pure electricity, a phenomenon that is used in therapeutic maneuverers in neurology such as transcranial magnetic stimulation (TMS) or tDCS (Transcranial Direct Current Stimulation) or bio photostimulation. The latter uses wave magnitudes close to those of the laser to stimulate or inhibit certain brain areas. The issue can reach such extremes that, for example, one of our colleagues at the Laurentian

---

| Page 455-463 Gaona et al., Archaeoacoustic investigation of a prehistoric cave site

2. Dubrov AP, Brown FA (1978) The geomagnetic field and life. Geomagnetobiology, Plenum Press, New York. p. 318.

3. Rajaram M, Mitra S (1981) Correlation between convulsive seizure and geomagnetic activity. Neurosci Lett 24: 187-191.

4. Michon AL, Persinger MA (1997) Experimental simulation of the effects of increased geomagnetic activity upon nocturnal seizures in epileptic rats. Neurosci Lett 224: 53-56.

University in Canada has carried out measurements of electrical differentials on the brains of cadavers, finding electrical activity obviously not produced by the brain itself, but as a consequence of physical energies around us.[5]

In order to understand this phenomenon, we must also talk about the energies that the brain itself generates at all times and that, since the beginning of the 20th century, the inventor of the electroencephalograph, Hans Berger, was able to demonstrate. Regarding this scientist, it should be added that he was ridiculed since the great scientific leaders of the time denied the possibility of electric fields being generated in the brain, with everything being a mere biochemical issue. This issue of negation by orthodox scientists' cultural constructs is still valid today.

The generation of energy in part of the brain that alters our environment translates into the alterations they cause in the random number generators.

Par example, specifically, large-scale animal mortality within a slaughterhouse factory was examined by Gaona et al.[6] for potential influence on the output of a random event generator. A number of intriguing effects were observed, and further theoretical interpretations were explored. Results previously obtained by Radin *et al.* determined that consciousness-correlated

---

5. Neural Tissues Filter Electromagnetic Fields: Investigating Regional Processing of Induced Current in Ex vivo Brain Specimens. Article in Biology and Medicine · January 2017. DOI: 10.4172/0974-8369.1000392. Rouleau, Nicholas. Persinger, Michael.

6. Gaona, J. M., Caswell, J. M., Tessaro, L. W. E. & Rouleau, N., Journal of Consciousness Exploration & Research| June 2014 | Volume 5 | Issue 5 | pp. 448-466 Transnational Exploratory FieldREG Investigation III: Statistical Anomalies in a Random Physical System Proximal to Large-Scale Animal Mortality

effects of a human operator on the growth of cultured cells appear to increase as time progresses.

Therefore, we propose a bidirectional interaction: our brains both receive and respond to physical stimuli from our surroundings and simultaneously "imprint" on the universe. This universe could act as a matrix, akin to a universal library or a collective consciousness, accessible to everyone.

The World as a Spiritual School

AJ Parr

Just as John Alexander pointed out, the BICS questions seemed to have ignored some of the lessons learned from NDE experiencers regarding time, the evolution of spirituality, and the role of the world as a spiritual school. Interestingly, the mediums rejected the assumptions made by the BICS questions and reiterated these lessons from NDErs: "This reality is a school to learn lessons of love."

A.- Five Major Conclusions

After analyzing the responses to the BICS questions, our main conclusions are:

FIRST:

The BICS project sheds light on the chief mysteries that have puzzled mankind since the dawn of time: Is there a God or a spirit world in charge of Earth? If so, why are there so many evils, wars, and calamities? Will humanity survive?

SECOND:

Despite their apparent differences, the different entities spoke in one voice. Like voices in a choir, they "sang the same song," transmitting the same big picture.

THIRD:

Human extinction is possible: "It can all go in smoke." However, The Other Side (TOS) has made a genuine effort to guide humanity.

The BICS project, which TOS directly inspired, offers solutions and steps we need to survive.

FOURTH:

Although humanity is in a "dark" phase, spiritual evolution has always been cyclical, alternating periods of light and darkness. Setbacks, calamities, and wars have always been integral to our overall development and crucial for our spiritual and moral progress.

FIFTH:

Earth is a place of learning and development, in which challenges, hardships, and calamities are opportunities for growth. They push individuals towards self-improvement and a deeper understanding of life's purposes. Obstacles allow us to learn, evolve, and advance towards higher moral and spiritual states.

B.- The Present State of Humankind

"Up till now, humankind has made unquestionable progress. Due to their intelligence, humans have achieved results never reached before regarding the sciences, arts, and material well-being. There is much progress yet to be made, however: they have yet to make charity, fraternity, and solidarity reign amongst them in order to assure their moral well-being (…). However, a change that is as radical as the one being prepared cannot be accomplished without commotion…"

Allan Kardec. Genesis

Although the present state of humankind denotes some kind of failure on behalf of humans or the Spirit World, this is not so. Autoextermination has an undeniable risk, but correct measures can avoid this.

TOS has tried to help, but humanity does not care to listen due to its loss of faith and belief in the spirit world. People choose fear, anger, and pride instead of wisdom and love. "Humans are thirsty, and the spirit world is the water needed; it is always present, but if humans will not drink, can they say that they were not helped?" To guide us, TOS has "dropped lanterns" like the Ten Commandments and "messengers inspired with vision and love," including Jesus and religious leaders, social reformers, and scientists such as the Dalai Lama. Billy Graham, Martin Luther King, Tesla, Edison, and Einstein, among others.

Moreover, to even help us further, they have also sent many trials and tribulations, including drastic geological changes like the Ice Age and even calamities designed to wake us up, such as the World Wars, 9/11, the Oklahoma Bombings and Jonestown, among others. Though hard to understand, this coincides with what Allan Kardec best expressed in:

"The Spirits Book," Part Three, Chapter VI. p. 412:

737. For what purpose does God inflict destructive calamities on humankind?

"To impel them to progress more quickly. Haven't we stated that destruction is necessary for the moral regeneration of spirits, who accomplish a new degree of perfection during each new existence? You must see the end in order to appreciate the results. You only judge such things from your point of view, and you regard such afflictions as calamities because of the injury they cause you. However, these hardships are often necessary in order to make things arrive at a better order more quickly and to accomplish in a few years what would otherwise require many centuries."

738. Couldn't God employ other methods instead of destructive calamities for improving humankind?

"Yes, and they are employed every day. Through the knowledge of good and evil, God has given each of you the means of progressing. However, humans do not take advantage of them; thus, it is necessary to afflict them in their pride and make them feel their own weakness." (The Spirits Book. Part Three, Chapter VI. p. 412)

C.- Earth is a School

"If they improved themselves during a lifetime and if they benefited from the lessons of experience, then upon returning, they will be instinctively better; matured in the school of suffering, and through work, their spirits will be stronger (...) It is in this way that each life is a step forward on the path of progress, a sort of a practical schooling."

Alan Kardec. Genesis

Everything seems to point out that "this reality is a school," more precisely, a "school of pain and suffering." Humans incarnate on Earth to learn, grow, and evolve under the supervision of TOS, which serves as a nonintrusive mentor. The learning journey is a continuous process of progression towards perfection through successive reincarnations in this experimentation field, learning center, or school of evolution, in which success and failure, as well as facing challenges and overcoming adversities, are integral to our spiritual and moral growth.

THE CURRICULUM OF LIFE

The curriculum offered by this universal school is not one of academics but of spiritual, moral, and emotional lessons. Despite its practically unlimited power, TOS restrains its interactions with humanity and opts for **gentle guidance** respecting the paramount principle of free will. This guidance is subtle, often manifesting as intuition, serendipitous events, or even challenges that, at first glance, seem insurmountable. Yet, each of these is a carefully placed stepping stone on the path to enlightenment and higher understanding. Thus, the soul must navigate through challenges, make choices, and face the consequences of those choices. This process is crucial for genuine spiritual growth.

NON-INTRUSIVE MENTORS

Viewing the world as a school helps us understand why TOS does not interfere much, ensuring that the lessons learned are deeply internalized rather than merely imparted.

Just as a teacher in a classroom provides the tools for learning but does not solve the problems for the student, the spirit world offers guidance, insights, and synchronicities that can help navigate life's complexities. However, they stop short of taking away the invaluable opportunity of learning through direct experience, gently steering the course of events to impart the lessons we need most, uniquely tailored to each individual's needs and stages of development.

The spirit world's role as a **gentle guide** rather than a direct intervener reinforces the educational nature of the earthly experience, providing support and nudges rather than overt actions. As Kardec explained in "The Medium's Book," "Humans must progress in everything by working for it. If everything were given to them entirely finished, how would that serve their intelligence? It would be like a school child whose homework was done by someone else."

LESSONS BASED ON FREE WILL

In their wisdom, the spirits understand that their role is not to lead us by the hand but to illuminate paths that we must choose to walk ourselves and thus design our lessons accordingly. Respecting the sacredness of free will and the necessity of personal endeavor in the journey of spiritual evolution, they create conditions and synchronicities—such as the inexplicable placement of a child at the scene of an accident who plays a crucial role in the rescue efforts—that serve as lessons and opportunities for human beings to act, choose, and thereby learn.

Each challenge we face, each joy we experience, and each hurdle we overcome is a lesson designed to foster our spiritual growth. The spirit world's role is to facilitate these lessons through subtle influences, ensuring that while they guide us toward growth opportunities, they do not deprive us of the invaluable experience of learning through our actions.

In sum, viewing the world as a school allows us to understand the inherent purpose in our trials and triumphs. Each moment is an opportunity to learn, grow, and move closer to our highest selves, with the spirit world as our ever-present, compassionate guide.

Regarding this, Allan Kardec expressed the following:

> **"Genesis: Miracles and Predictions According to Spiritism". Chapter 1 p. 51-52**
>
> Would you criticize a father for repeating the same lessons to his children ten times or a hundred times if they did not profit from them? Why would God do any less than such a father? Why would God not, from time to

time, send special messengers to humans, entrusted with reminding them of their duties and leading them back onto the right path when they wander from it, and opening the eyes of intelligence for those who have closed them, just as more advanced cultures send missionaries to those that are less evolved?

The Spirits teach no other morality than that of Christ for the simple reason that no other is better. However, what use would their teachings be if they told us only what we already knew? The same might be said of Christ's morality, which had been taught by Socrates and Plato five-hundred years earlier and in almost identical terms; and of all moralists who have repeated the same thing in all sorts of tones and under all sorts of forms. Very well! The Spirits have come simply to increase the number of moralists, but with the difference that, manifesting themselves far and wide, they make themselves heard in the hut as well as in the palace by the uneducated as well as the educated. (The Spirits Book Part Three, Chapter VI, P. 412

BICS Challenge Report

Consciousness and the Informational Universe

Isabelle Chauffeton Saavedra

What is consciousness? This million-dollar question has baffled the scientific community for as long as neuroscience has existed.

Is it the byproduct of brain activity? "An emergent phenomenon like wetness or solidity?" as theoretical physicist Sean Caroll once answered me in one of his live Facebook chats, or could it be one of the most essential inherent properties of the Universe (Multiverse)?

There is no way to answer this fundamental question in a short paragraph, but it is important to note that consciousness is at the forefront of everything. Without consciousness, any and all scientific theories do not exist. "I think therefore I am," said Descartes in his attempt to grasp the logic behind our reasoning and state of being. What we call consciousness today is, in fact, the collection of information that our brain is aware of: information about how warm it is outside, the color of the sky, how it feels to be sad or happy, the nature of quarks and the possible theory of the original inflationary expansion of the universe. When our brain is in a deep state of sleep or incapacitated, like in a coma, science has determined that we are "unconscious" without "consciousness."

What does that mean? In today's neuroscience terms, we have no access to information (by our brain) without consciousness. You may have heard this phrasing: If a tree falls in the forest, and no one is present to listen to the tree fall, there is no sound. This philosophical sentence seems to have originated from the 1910 book *Physics* by Charles Riborg Mann and George Ransom Twiss.

However, much earlier, in 1710, the same sort of reasoning appeared in George Berkeley's 1710 work, "A Treatise Concerning the Principles of Human Knowledge." Both argue that without a thinking/conscious human, reality does not exist.

If we play along this reasoning, one could ask, what is a sound? A sound is a vibration that propagates in the air (or another medium) and can be heard by one's ears. The vibration, the wave that travels through the ambient nature, hits our eardrums with sound energy, kinetic energy from the air created by the sound wave. That sound energy is turned into electromagnetic signals traveling through our brain axons to our neurons in charge of interpreting them as sound. So, if no one is in the forest (or… if no one is "conscious" in the forest), there will be no interpretation of the vibration of the air created by the tree falling.

However, does it mean the sound wave does not exist? Arguably, as modern scientists and philosophers have long debated this question, would the absence of recording or awareness of our surroundings from our human brains mean the absence of the existence of those surroundings? No one has the answer. At best, this is what science calls conjecture, and the debate can continue forever.

Let us look at consciousness from a different angle—not from the angle where it is what makes the universe real, but from the point of view from which it encompasses the sum total of information about the universe (or even the multiverse). Since this scientific hypothesis cannot be proven or disproven into a theory either way because of our conjecture problem, we can use it as our framework.

It is important to note that information is often associated with or synonym of the knowledge, the interpretation of data, the output of analyzing and conceptualizing and not the source itself. Again, since everything has been linked to our awareness and filtering brain, the definitions of information and consciousness are tainted with one side of the conjecture: the hypothesis that we need to be aware for the source of everything to exist.

However, quantum mechanics has long proven that this could not be farther from the truth. In quantum physics, the subatomic world follows rules that are simply not deterministic. In a quantum system, all its possible outcomes exist until the system is observed; then, the equation collapses into one and one outcome only, while all the others can no longer be part of the observer's reality. In other words, quantum mechanics shows that although the role of an observer is paramount in the outcome of an experiment, all the outcomes exist regardless of the observer before being observed.

The conjecture still exists, as to witness these extraordinary properties of the quantum world, we still have to write and interpret those equations. However, it makes our concept of a framework for consciousness, which is the sum total of all information (all the outcomes), more robust.

Let us continue on this path using this framework. Suppose consciousness is the sum total of all the information. Regardless of space and time and any dimension the universe (multiverse) is built upon, consciousness must contain all that information and its source. Thus, consciousness is not an emergent phenomenon but a real, intrinsic part of the fabric of the universe.

Moreover, suppose consciousness is the source of all knowledge, past, present, and future. In that case, we, mere observers, can only have a very reductive view of its entirety in our everyday life, as we constantly collapse all of its outcomes into one: the one we are observing, the one we are aware of at a specific point in space and time, with the capacity our brain has acquired to do so. By collapsing that one specific outcome, we are detaching ourselves from the infinite number of other possibilities, outcomes, and the rest of the universe's information.

However, if we follow that path, within that framework of consciousness, as the cat in Schrödinger's box is both alive and dead at the same time, as long as no one has observed the decaying of the one Nitrogen-13 atom inside the box, our lives may very well be happening in many different ways simultaneously as long as we do not entangle ourselves with one particular outcome. Moreover, the information of those lives exists in the field of all potentialities. The novel Dark Matter by Blake Crouch is an excellent illustration of this theory.

Now, what is that sum total of information? How does it work, where is it stored? In physics, there are four main force fields: the gravity force field, strong and weak nuclear force fields, and the electromagnetic force fields. Force fields exert a force on particles within that field, which requires energy. For example, we know magnets have magnetic fields, and if you place a paper clip close to one, it will be attracted by the magnet. The force field acts upon the paper clip long before the clip touches the magnet. Fields can be vector fields or scalar fields. Vector fields have magnitude and direction (I am traveling 60 miles an hour towards the North), scalar fields only have magnitude (a map of temperatures across the US at every point shows the magnitude of the temperature at each point, but there is no direction/movement associated with it)

Bear with me as I take you through this framework blueprint:

In the same way, there is a graviton (the smallest particle, a quantum of gravity), an electron, a proton, and even an inflaton (to illustrate a particle of the inflationary expansion field, as physicist Brian Greene denotes in his book "The Hidden Reality" Parallel Universes and the Deep Laws of the Cosmos), I would like to postulate that there is a particle of information called the "information."

If consciousness is a vector field, it has magnitude (amount of energy) and direction (going one way or another). So technically, we should be able to quantitatively measure the amount and the movement of information within that field. I am not talking about information in a binary computer system where 1s and 0s reign; as we know, this is already quantifiable. By information, I mean any kind of information, regardless of the state of things and people on Earth. Whether you are interested in the T-Cr borealis supernova that all astronomers are waiting for to happen before this September 2024 (which can be measured in a binary way), or whether you are wondering if your comatose loved one has a way to know that you love him (nothing can measure that yet); all of this, is part of the information field and each quantum of information ("information") has an effect (magnitude) and a (direction) to where the information is traveling.

This is precisely what the Global Consciousness Project has tried to illustrate at Princeton University using random number generators tracking deviations in randomness in their FieldREGSs worldwide after major events such as a football World Cup or the death of Lady Di. This particular research only looked at the magnitude and not the direction. However, if we could think of those random number generators and their position on the planet, or even our brains for that matter, as receivers within that field, we could very easily think of a field of information that not only has magnitude but direction for it to be detected at many different locations. Today, Dr. Melvin Morse regularly uses a random number generator while working with psychic mediums to document any deviation in the field of randomness. Although more studies need to happen on the subject, the preliminary results are encouraging, pointing to the fact that neuroscientists and physicists need to explore this framework of consciousness with more rigorous scientific methods.

How does all this relate to mediumship? For lack of a better word, mediumship is simply the intuitive way to illustrate that the information is active and not passive. Our brains are constantly bathing in the information field, most of which we cannot seem to access because of the deterministic nature of our Newtonian reality. However, the psychic experiments we do, training our brains to not only react to the magnitude but also the direction of information within this framework of consciousness, force us to look at consciousness not as a by-product of our brains nor as an emergent phenomenon of our very own existence, but with a bird's eye view into Quantum Indeterminacy. It nudges our quest for understanding toward considering consciousness an actual intrinsic part of the universe (multiverse). This field may be the building blocks of all realities, including the one we create for ourselves.

Considerations

AJ Parr

The coincidences found in the different answers prove that, beyond the message conveyed, there seems to be solid evidence of true communication between humans and the spiritual world, something science has not accepted to this date.

Moreover, the alignment of the US team's findings with those of the other international teams could serve as a global validation of the possibility and reality of communication with the spiritual realm. This alignment would not only shift this field of research from speculative philosophy to empirical study but also pave the way for profound considerations and potential impacts on humanity.

As a direct consequence of the present study, we recommend further successive contact with the spiritual world to better understand the mysteries surrounding consciousness and its post-mortem persistence.

This is why we urge BICS to follow up on this project with further efforts to methodically contact The Other Side under controlled conditions by the different international teams. This could give birth to an ongoing project designed to bring a deeper understanding of spiritual and psychological matters, capable of revolutionizing psychology, neuroscience, and philosophy, offering empirical data on what has traditionally been speculative.

Also worth considering is the possibility of developing new methodologies to allow consistent communication with the spiritual world under controlled conditions, thus making it a part of empirical science. After all, as TOS explained, the future development of technological advancements capable of facilitating this communication is also possible. This could involve advanced AI, quantum computing, or entirely new fields of technology focusing on the interface between physical and spiritual realms.

Undoubtedly, verified communication with the spiritual realm could significantly influence world religions and spiritual beliefs. It could validate certain beliefs, challenge others, and fundamentally reshape humanity's spiritual landscape. The transition from faith to empirical evidence in spiritual matters could spark a renaissance in spiritual and religious expression, fostering a new era of interfaith dialogue and exploration.

In conclusion, the scientific establishment of communication with the spiritual realm can usher in an era of profound change, touching every aspect of human life. From the most intimate personal beliefs to the broadest societal structures, the impact of this breakthrough would be both transformative and enduring, challenging humanity to navigate a future where the spiritual and material worlds are irrevocably intertwined.

An Urgent Message for Humanity

Final Conclusions

Melvin L. Morse, MD

The spirit world has presented an urgent message to us: We are at a crossroads in human development. Our failures to love one another have escalated to the point where we face self-extinction.

The message is urgent and unmistakable. It is easy to ignore, as we have been presented with so many scenarios of doom and gloom, from nuclear holocausts to warnings from scientists about climate change incompatible with human life, over the past decades.

Consider this: Robert Bigelow funded this inquiry into the spiritual world concerning humanity's seemingly lack of spiritual progress over the past 150-plus years. We presented these questions as numbers to 19 different mediums living in various areas of the United States. All nineteen mediums were unanimous in transmitting this urgent and surprising message to humanity: Learn to love or face extinction.

One surprising message from the spirit realm is that death is the great engine of spiritual development. We fear death, as it represents the loss of everything we know to be real. Even if there is a life after death, we often fear the loss of loved ones or the loss of our individual consciousness and all that we have learned, strived for, and achieved throughout our lives. However, the message transmitted by the mediums that they often did not understand or even agree with is that death is a time of respite and reflection, a catalyst for spiritual growth and reunion.

When we realize that this reality is a school, a place for us to learn lessons of love, we can understand this message that death is not to be feared but heralds a reunion with the unconditional love of the universe and the spiritual family that supports us, the spiritual roots that we are perpetually entwined with.

These lessons are often harsh and challenging for us to comprehend. So often, we cry out, asking why bad things happen to good people. The spirit world answers that bad things are, in fact, our challenges, our lessons, and even our rewards for being good people. As we rise to a certain level of spiritual competency and begin to understand our lessons of love, we are often immediately confronted with new ones. These lessons can take lifetimes to learn.

Another surprising message was the unity between the spiritual world and this reality. Again and again, we were told that we are the spiritual world and that they evolve with us. Humans often separate the spiritual world into various sectors; one common sentiment is that one can be spiritual without being religious. However, the spirit world reminded us repeatedly that religion and spirituality cannot easily be separated. When we asked the spirit world the second BICS question, which addressed the specific ways the spirit world has tried to help us, the first response was a reference to the Ten Commandments.

This message is for members of all faiths and creeds. Our mediums forcefully transmitted the message that this world is a spiritual reality and cannot be easily divided into categories such as Islam, Christianity, New Age, or Zen Buddhism. Each represents a point of light tailored to illuminate a specific lesson of love for a given culture and population.

As scientists, we know that the message transmitted through the mediums resonates with our understanding of the nature of reality. Our minds and brains create this reality. Time, space, and even individual colors are products of our minds and brains. Consciousness is not. Consciousness uses our brains to develop a personal consciousness, and now we understand why: we require an individual consciousness to learn our unique lessons of love.

When our brains die, the personal consciousness that we have spent a lifetime cultivating must indeed die with them. However, all we have accomplished and learned are bits of information, information eternally stored within the fabric of reality, the non-local reality described by theoretical physicists as real. The term "non-local" means that it is everywhere and nowhere all at once. Our mediums told us that this non-local reality is imbued with unconditional love for us, which awaits us after our lessons are completed. Our consciousness continues, perhaps moving on to a new brain, which will result in a new individual consciousness, yet its link with the cluster of information that makes us unique and personal is eternal. The brain is simply an antenna that allows us to create and exist within this specialized reality with a specific purpose unique to each of us.

The four BICS questions essentially ask about the nature of spiritual progress and who is to blame if humanity is not progressing spiritually. The answers challenged the basic assumptions of the questions, which are that war, conflict, adversity, and strife represent spiritual failures. Instead, we are firmly instructed that they are our lessons, our opportunities to learn, grow, and sometimes fail.

The spirit world surrounds us, encourages us, inspires us, suffers with us, and evolves with us. Grief, suffering, physical and emotional pain, the horrors of violence and war, and the casual cruelties of everyday life are all spiritual events that we must either transcend or be crushed and destroyed. We are the students in this complex school, taught often unbearable lessons of love; we are not the teachers, nor can we understand the lesson plans.

All of this typically happens through individuals. Enlightened religious leaders such as Jesus Christ or Lao Tzu inspired scientists such as those who made the discoveries that led to the scientific age of Enlightenment, and ordinary people who spread joy and love throughout their daily routines are the typical movers and shakers of spiritual progress. Sometimes, more dramatic interventions are needed, such as the creation of an Ice Age, to move humans around the globe to further the progress of civilization. Such interventions often occur on an individual basis, such as a person getting a new job in another community, which presents specific opportunities to learn lessons of love.

The spirit world, the I Am of the great religions, and the individual angels and spirit guides that surround us mostly play the role of parents observing their children, for example, learning to walk. There is considerable repetition and repeated failure before the child can run and progress to the next level.

The answer to the 4 BICS questions was clear: Stop worrying about a lack of spiritual progress and realize that if humanity is extinct, the school is closed, and no further lessons can be learned. We have already been given all the spiritual guidance we need, starting with the Ten Commandments and the teachings of the World's great religions. We must listen and act, or we will lose all our progress over the past several hundred thousand years.

About the Authors

DR. MELVIN MORSE

ISSC President / Senior Chief Researcher

Dr. Melvin Morse is a Neuroscientist and former Professor of Pediatrics at the University of Washington. His peers have repeatedly recognized him as one of America's Best Doctors. He published the world's first prospective study of near-death experiences (NDEs) in children who survived cardiac arrest at Seattle Children's Hospital. He is the President of the Institute for the Scientific Study of Consciousness (ISSC), selected by the Bigelow Institute for Consciousness Studies as one of the BICS Challenge Program Teams. He received the Warcollier Prize for consciousness research. He is the subject of numerous documentaries and has appeared on TV shows, from Larry King to Oprah.

http://www.melvinmorsemd.com

DR. RAYMOND MOODY

ISSC Consulting Researcher

Dr. Raymond Moody is a philosopher, psychologist, and physician widely recognized as a pioneer in near-death experience (NDE) research. He coined the term "near-death experience" in his bestselling 1975 book Life After Life. Moody's work has profoundly influenced the medical, psychiatric, and theological fields, igniting interest in consciousness and its relationship to death. He continues to write and lecture on issues related to NDEs, the afterlife, and the exploration of consciousness.

https://www.lifeafterlife.com

COL (R) JOHN B. ALEXANDER

ISSC Consulting Researcher

Colonel John Alexander is a retired U.S. Army officer known for his work in non-lethal weapons. He is deeply interested in unconventional areas like paranormal phenomena and consciousness studies.

He has been involved in exploring psychotronic, telepathic, and other psychic capabilities.

https://www.johnbalexander.com/

DR. JOSÉ MIGUEL GAONA

ISSC Consulting Forensic Psychiatrist

José Miguel is a Specialist in forensic neuropsychiatry; he has trained at Harvard in non-invasive brain techniques and served as a visiting Professor at Laurentian University, working with Michael Persinger, MD. He has a degree in theology from Navarro University. He serves as a consultant responsible for the area of mental health during the Bosnian war for the NGO Doctors of the World—medical director of the Neurosalus Institute, Spain's premiere neuropsychiatric treatment facility.

https://josemiguelgaona.com

ISABELLE CHAUFFETON-SAAVEDRA

ISSC Senior Designer Experiential Studies

Isabelle has authored three books on scientific mediumship and pioneered using mediumship to contact a (living) comatose hospitalized patient. She is the CEO of a successful event planning company whose clients include Microsoft, agencies specialized in corporate incentive travel and medical conventions, and the first French astronaut to fly on the Discovery Shuttle."

http://www.survivalofconsciousness.com/

AJ PARR (ÁLVARO PARRA PINTO)

ISSC Senior Research Associate/Consciousness Researcher

AJ is an Internationally recognized spiritual journalist and best-selling author. He has spent three decades researching comparative religions, human consciousness, the origins of language, and near-death experiences. He has written over twenty books on spirituality and hosts the AJ Parr Spiritual Journalist YouTube channel, where he features interviews with NDE survivors, mediums, and virtually every major consciousness researcher. He is the founder and CEO of the publishing company for independent authors Grapevine Books.

https://www.youtube.com/@AJParrNDE

Index of Topics

Allen Kardek, pp. 124f, 172

All knowledge, p. 12

Altering stream of electron flow, pp. 13, 45

Angels, p. 32; names of, 50

Angry earthbound spirit, influence of, p. 94

Asking for help is needed for help to be given, p. 77

Balance of "good" and "bad" needed for growth, p. 95

Benzene ring, p. 64

Bilocation, pp. 47, 63, 103

Blue beings of universal consciousness, p. 49

"But we do", p. 47

Calamities foster spiritual growth, p. 72

Cause and effect (karma), p. 28

Choosing Love, pp. 116f

Choosing one of many realities that will collapse by observing it, p. 191

Conditions and synchronicities are created by The Other Side, pp. 102, 120f, 186

Connect to love for guidance, pp. 70, 110

Connect to spirit, p. 81

Consciousness evolves, p. 76

Christ's teachings – "no other that is better," p. 187

Death, war, pp. 34f, 64, 88ff, 112, 115; 911, p. 197

Deceit, bad spirits win by, p. 69

Design of the Earth plane ("nature of the world"), pp. 68, 197

Destructive spirits, two sets of, p. 94

Discerning the spirits, p. 157

Dreams, pp. 84, 86, 102

Dropping lanterns, pp. 79, 183

Duality created by spirit, p. 82

Earth's unique position in the Universe, p. 88

Energy vampires, p. 92

Epic battle between forces of good and evil, pp. 58f, 94F, 108

Evil spirits, influence of, p. 118

Evolving further through difficult trials, pp. 72, 95f

Experience brings learning and growth, p. 98

Failure, p. 34

Free will, pp, 96ff, 107

Frequencies: 1/f, p. 66 – the physical signature of consciousness; 110 Hz, p. 177

Full trance medium, p. 48

Future event kept secret, p. 151; devastation p. 167; like earthquake, p. 169

Gaza, p. 115

God, p. 124; God spot on brain, p. 127; God module, pp. 132f;

Great awakening, p. 69

Guidance available, pp. 70, 149, 156

Hopeful words for a good outcome for humanity, pp. 69, 71, 85, 107, 155

How the spirit world has helped humanity, pp. 79, 83f, 86ff

Human progress, p. 107

I Am, pp. 33, 50f, 89, 97, 102, 114, 153, 166

Illusion, the world is, p. 84

Inspiration, p. 88, through meditation, pp. 83f

Inter-dimensional beings, p. 51

Jesus, "a prophet, brought to earth to advance mankind", pp. 79, 86

Learn to love or face extinction, pp. 121, 197

Life-review, p. 73

Lightworkers, pp. 113f

Local and universal presence simultaneously, p 51

Materialism, p. 125

Meditation, p. 8

Mediums, kinds of, p. 55

Mediumship, p. 11

Mission (to learn) to love, p. 106

Near-death experiences, pp. 2f, 62, 85

Non-local, p. 199

Nuclear weapons, p. 169

Obstacles to stimulate growth, pp. 182ff

Oneness in Nature, the human model, pp. 68, 71

Oneness of the physical and the spiritual worlds, pp. 77, 81f

Political lies, p. 69

Portal to other realities, p. 106

Powerful dark leadership, pp. 69f

Present state of humankind, p. 182

Progress through failure p. 68

Quantum envisioning possibility, p. 191

Quantum Indeterminacy, p. 194

Random number generator, pp. 14f, 193

Realer than real, p. 63

Reincarnation, spiritual progress through, pp. 27f, 90, 93, 172, 183f

Religion, failure of, p. 77, 79; 34, 84, 86; God's comment on being falsely described, p.114

Remedy, pp. 150f

Remote retroactive prayer, p. 126

Self-correction, p. 75

Safe signals, p. 110

Seeing through the skin, p. 61

Self-inflicted extinction, risk of, pp. 73f

Soldiers to angels, p. 154

Source breaking off pieces of Itself, p. 82

Space and time, p. 11

Spiritual inspiration behind human progress, p. 52

Spiritual growth perspective, p. 114

Spiritual progress through free will in duality, pp. 28, 69

Struggle for survival no longer all-consuming, p. 113

Suffering, God allows for learning purposes, p. 98

T-Cr borealis Supernova, p. 193

Technology, the good and the bad aspects, p. 85

Temporary subjugation of a culture results in more speedy evolution, p. 154

Ten Commandments, pp. 60, 78, 86

The Other Side, p. 124

Thermometer, pp. 65, 80

Thousand year view, pp. 58, 83

Time, the ability to stop, p. 87

Time and space, pp. 123, 132

Tragedies create spiritual progress, pp. 89, 183

Unconditional Love, p. 123

Ultimate goal of the Universe, p. 86

"Universe is math," p. 128

Universal interconnectivity, pp. 99, 103

Upheaval to come is necessary, p. 109

Veil is thinning, p. 108

"what he is seeking is also seeking him," p. 103

Wars to end when, p. 154

Worst ever condition of spiritual awareness is now; p. 72

110 Hz, p. 177

This Book was Published
in September, 2024, by:

*Bigelow Institute of Consciousness Studies
Challenge Grant Recipient*

FINAL REPORT

EDITED BY:
DR. MELVIN MORSE
http://www.melvinmorsemd.com

PRODUCTION AND LAYOUT:
AJ PARR
ajparrbooks@gmail.com

GRAPEVINE BOOKS
First Edition 2024
Copyright © ISSC 2024
ALL RIGHTS RESERVED

Printed in Great Britain
by Amazon